ON GREAT WHITE WINGS

*"We bowed our heads before the mystery
of it and then lifted our eyes with a new
feeling in our souls that seemed to link
us all, and hope sprang eternal for the great
new future of the world."*

— Mary M. Parker, after
seeing the first airplane fly
over Chicago in 1910

ON GR

By Fred E.C. Culick and Spencer Dunmore

*Featuring archival photographs by Orville and Wilbur Wright
and contemporary photographs by Peter Christopher and Dan Patterson*

EAT WHITE WINGS

The Wright Brothers and the Race for Flight

A HYPERION / MADISON PRESS BOOK

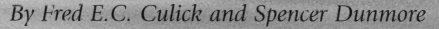

First published in the United States by
Hyperion
77 West 66th Street
New York, New York
10023-6298

First U.S. Edition, 2001
1 3 5 7 9 10 8 6 4 2

Library of Congress Cataloging-in-Publication
Data is on file.

ISBN 0-7868-6686-1

Produced by Madison Press Books
1000 Yonge Street
Toronto, Ontario
Canada M4W 2K2

Printed and bound in Italy

Onlookers cheer as Orville Wright flies near Berlin in September 1909.

(Above) Stone markers at Kitty Hawk, North Carolina, show the distances of the Wright brothers' first flights. (Opposite) The Wright Brothers National Memorial at Kill Devil Hills was dedicated in 1932.

CONTENTS

# Introduction

"The Wrights' powered aircraft was the first great invention of the twentieth century."

It was a scene the Wright brothers could scarcely have imagined. Inside a vast wind tunnel used for testing helicopters and high-speed aircraft stood an exact, aerodynamic replica of their 1903 Flyer — complete with a lifelike dummy of Orville at the controls. It was February 19, 1999, and my colleagues and I from the Los Angeles Section of the American Institute of Aeronautics and Astronautics (AIAA) were at the NASA Ames Research Center at Moffett Field, California. Together with the press and thousands joining us via the World Wide Web, we watched as the Flyer was hoisted one hundred feet in a stand called the "sting."

The two weeks of testing that followed were the culmination of a twenty-year dream that began, strangely enough, shortly after a fire tore through the San Diego Aerospace Museum in 1978. The fire destroyed a replica of the Flyer that had originally been built by the AIAA in the early fifties, so our Los Angeles-based group decided to build not one, but two new replicas. One would be constructed to actually fly, and the other would serve as a full-scale wind-tunnel model.

The original goal of the Wright Flyer Project, as we called ourselves, had been to build an operational replica of the 1903 Flyer — one that would be faithful to the original but that could be flown repeatedly and safely by several different pilots. Our plan had been to give public demonstrations, accurately re-creating that first powered flight so dramatically captured in one of the most famous photographs of the twentieth century (see pages 76–77). But we discovered that the original Flyer wasn't an easy aircraft to fly; in fact, it was downright dangerous — as the Wrights well understood. A lot of Orville and Wilbur's later work was an attempt to solve the design problems that plagued their first powered aircraft.

My colleagues and I soon realized that to create a safe flying replica, some design revisions would have to be made. But how much — or how little — would we have to alter the Wrights' original design? To answer that question, we would have to understand as completely as possible all the aerodynamic characteristics of the original Flyer. And that brings us back to 1999 and the NASA wind-tunnel tests.

The Wrights' powered aircraft was the first great invention of the twentieth century, and the story of the Wrights' activities during their most intense working period, 1899–1905, has been told many times. But the true technical characteristics of their airplanes have remained a puzzle — until now. With the data obtained from the full-scale wind-tunnel tests (combined with our earlier tests using scale models), members of the Wright Flyer Project have been able to analyze — and, finally, to understand — the aeronautical characteristics of the 1903 Flyer. Through computer and test aircraft simulations, we now know what it was like to fly the first piloted and powered aircraft. And we hope that this knowledge, distilled in features throughout the book, will provide a new understanding of how brilliantly the Wright brothers triumphed on that fateful December day in 1903.

— *Fred Culick*

(Opposite) Anchored securely in the sting, the re-created Flyer is now ready for testing.

The wind gained strength moment by moment as it whipped across the bleak dunes, blowing stinging showers of sand in the faces of the three men. They ignored it, concentrating entirely on preventing the glider, a sizable biplane, more than seventeen feet tip to tip, from being torn out of their hands. Its structures creaked, complaining like a boat in a storm. They had to hang on tightly, for the glider seemed to be coming to life in the blow, straining to get away, to be free, to fly.

The men glanced at one another. They nodded, agreeing. It was time. The wind was strong but strong winds were the reason they had come to this place, weren't they? For their work they needed powerful winds. Yes, the stomach lurched a little at the thought. But there was no alternative. The control system worked. Hadn't they tested it thoroughly in dozens of flights, standing on the ground and manipulating the controls

by means of cords to the wings and tail? They had acquired a certain skill. A tug here. Another there. She reacted obediently every time, swooping, soaring, doing precisely what they asked of her. No question about it: the wing-warping system and the front-mounted tail unit provided total control of the craft.

So there wasn't any reason to delay any longer, was there? It had already been agreed that Wilbur would go first. It was his right. He had been the architect of the entire enterprise, shaping the craft every hesitant step along the way. His younger brother Orville had been a vital member of the team, but essentially a follower rather than a leader.

With a curt, no-nonsense nod at Orville, Wilbur clambered onto the lower wing and settled himself as comfortably as he could, hooking his toes behind the rear spar, reaching for the lever that controlled the nose-mounted elevator. The wind drummed on the taut fabric covering of the wings, a tern

FOREWORD # To Ride the WIND

"If the plan will enable me to remain in the air for practice by the hour instead of by the second, I hope to acquire skill sufficient to overcome the difficulties inherent in flight."

— Wilbur Wright to Octave Chanute, October 1900

squawked as it flew overhead, perhaps puzzled by the sight of the men and their odd-looking bird. Orville and Bill Tate, their helper, took up their positions at each wing tip. They nodded. Now! They ran forward a few steps. The glider fairly leapt into the air as the boisterous wind swept over the wings. In a moment the glider was climbing, borne up on the wind as if it were no heavier than a feather.

Clinging to the lower wing, Wilbur watched wide-eyed as the world unrolled beneath him. He experienced a moment's alarm as the craft banged and thumped and skidded like a cart on a rough track. He had expected it to be much smoother. The wind roared in his ears. He glimpsed Orville and Bill below, trotting on the sand, the control cords still in their hands. The ground dropped away, tilting, the sand stretching away to the sea. For the first time, he experienced the wonder of flight, of riding the air. An exquisite sensation, like nothing he had ever known before. Then . . . alarm! The glider bucked, up and down, plunging, rising, while the wind bellowed at him. Surely it was strong enough to rip the control cords out of Orville's and Bill's hands. The two of them were still there, looking up at him, one yelling something that couldn't be heard because of the wind. Suddenly, the sand tilted like a picture knocked off balance. As if startled, the glider abruptly rose. Then plunged. Then rose again. A bucking bronco of the air.

Wilbur had a terrifying feeling that he was about to be tossed bodily out of the glider. Clinging even more tightly to the struts, he yelled to the ground team to bring the glider down. He gesticulated. Nodded. Hands reached for the cords. Wilbur felt the glider's nose jerk down. Relieved, he saw the sand sliding up to meet him. The last few seconds of the flight were wonderfully smooth. In a moment, the skids made contact. A gentle thump. A spray of sand hit him in the face. He breathed again. He had flown. He had ridden the wind. And nothing would ever be quite the same again.

With hands clasped tightly to the wing struts and body braced against the fierce North Carolina winds, Wilbur soars above the sand dunes at Kitty Hawk in the Wright brothers' 1902 glider.

A Dream of WINGS

"Isn't it astonishing that all these secrets have been preserved for so many years just so that we could discover them!"

— Orville Wright, June 7, 1903

Singular individuals, those two brothers from Dayton, Ohio. Name of Wright. Wilbur, the elder, was born in 1867; Orville, four years later. Most of their contemporaries saw them as typical businessmen, invariably garbed in business suits of somber hue with high, stiff collars. Wilbur's bald head and Orville's walrus mustache completed the picture of conventionality. Who could have guessed that these altogether average-looking men would change the world? Yet that's precisely what they did when they invented the airplane.

The two brothers ran a bicycle shop on West Third Street in Dayton, earning a moderately good living. They never spent a penny unwisely, they didn't smoke or drink, and they had practically nothing to do with the opposite sex, except in the person of their sister Katharine and her friends. The brothers met many of them but no romances ensued. The young ladies must have found the brothers a mystery, two eminently eligible bachelors who seemed far more interested in aeronautical matters than almost anything else.

There's no doubt the ladies also found them dull and straitlaced, but in this they would have been mistaken. A keen sense of humor lurked behind the brothers' serious demeanor. Their world was their family and within its confines they were

(Opposite) Wilbur, left, and Orville pose informally on the steps of the rear porch at Seven Hawthorn Street in June 1909.

fractious and demonstrative, often spending entire evenings loudly arguing some point of contention. They had two older brothers — Reuchlin, born in 1861, and Lorin, born a year later. Their sister Katharine was born in 1874.

Undoubtedly, the Wright brothers' most striking characteristic was their extraordinary compatibility. Despite their arguing, their devotion to each other never wavered. In later years, Wilbur wrote: "From the time we were little children, my brother Orville and myself lived together, played together, worked together, and in fact, thought together. We usually owned all of our toys in common, talked over our thoughts and aspirations so that nearly everything that was done in our lives has been the result of conversations, suggestions, and discussions between us." Their father, Bishop Milton Wright of the Church of the United Brethren in Christ, said they were as inseparable as twins.

They bore only a passing resemblance to each other, although both men possessed the blue-gray eyes and aggressive, determined jawline of the Wrights. Of the two, Wilbur seemed the more decisive, while Orville tended to be easygoing. Wilbur could be withdrawn and introspective. Orville was something of a prankster. Wilbur had little interest in clothes; by contrast, Orville cared for his wardrobe and always protected his suits by wearing sleeve cuffs and an apron when he was in the bicycle shop.

They argued constantly, vehemently, yet at times their minds seemed interconnected. One night, they returned home after working late at the shop, Orville arriving first. He was already in bed when Wilbur came in. Wilbur had neglected to lock the front door, a most uncommon occurrence, and Orville pointed out the oversight. While Wilbur went to bolt the door, Orville, already half asleep, became convinced that his brother had blown out the gas light in his room instead of turning it off. Upon investigation, the brothers discovered that the gas had indeed been left on. If not for Orville's presentiment, the invention of the airplane might have been left to others!

The brothers' interest in flight went back a long way, to 1877, when their father returned from a business trip with a gift for them — a toy helicopter made of cork, bamboo, and paper, its twin propellers powered by twisted rubber bands. Fascinated, the boys were soon building helicopters of their own — and discovering an important truth: making them bigger didn't necessarily improve them. In fact, it usually had the opposite effect. Why? They pondered the question. They enjoyed pondering just as they enjoyed dismantling machines and discovering what made them tick. It came easily to them, no doubt a talent inherited from their mother, Susan Koerner Wright, the daughter of a designer of fine carriages and farm wagons, an intensely practical woman who seemed capable of fixing anything from household appliances to toys. Invention came easily to her sons. Wilbur created a paper-

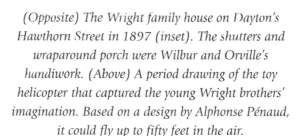

(Opposite) The Wright family house on Dayton's Hawthorn Street in 1897 (inset). The shutters and wraparound porch were Wilbur and Orville's handiwork. (Above) A period drawing of the toy helicopter that captured the young Wright brothers' imagination. Based on a design by Alphonse Pénaud, it could fly up to fifty feet in the air.

folding device. He and Orville made woodcuts and prints and, later, a lathe. Orville published a newspaper and built a press to handle print jobs for local merchants.

During this period, Wilbur was also a keen sportsman. But at the age of eighteen, he took a terrible blow in the face during a game of shinny. In one catastrophic instant, he lost most of his upper teeth and a number of lower ones. Extensive dental and medical work were required to repair the damage. He sank into a severe depression made worse by the deteriorating health of his mother. For several years, he devotedly nursed her, rarely leaving the house. There is no telling how long that state of affairs might have lasted had Orville, then sixteen, not asked his older brother for help with a printing press he was building. Wilbur's depression lifted and he began to take an interest in life again.

When Wilbur was twenty-two, his mother died of what has been variously described as pleurisy and consumption. At the time, Orville was working for a Dayton printer and had begun publication of a weekly paper, *West Side News*. Wilbur contributed items of local interest. The paper did well for about a year, after which it disappeared, overwhelmed by competition from the large Dayton dailies.

The Wrights abandoned publishing without regret. A new interest had taken their fancy — bicycles. The industry was undergoing a revolution as the ungainly high-wheeler bicycles (known as penny-farthings in England) rapidly gave

Bishop Milton Wright *c. 1900*

Mrs. Susan Wright *c. 1885*

Katharine Wright *c. 1900*

At Home on Hawthorn Street

Wilbur was four years old when Bishop Wright moved the family into the house on Hawthorn Street in West Dayton, Ohio, in April 1871. Orville was born in the upstairs front bedroom five months later. Katharine, the only surviving daughter, was born three years later to the day.

Although the Wrights were not rich, the house on Hawthorn Street was comfortable enough by the standards of the day. And the well-furnished home was often filled with visitors and spirited discussions (below, left). Milton and Susan Wright were warm, loving, and protective parents who encouraged close relationships among their children. Bishop Wright had an extensive library, and the children's intellectual curiosity was fostered. But it was Orville and Wilbur's mother — not their father — who was responsible for the brothers' lifelong love of tinkering and experimentation. Susan Wright had spent time in her father's carriage shop as a young child and now put her considerable mechanical aptitude to use by designing and building simple household appliances for herself and toys for her children. Her two youngest sons inherited her extraordinary ability to visualize the operation of a mechanism *before* it was even constructed.

way to "safety bicycles" with equal-sized, rubber-tired, chain-driven wheels. The new bikes were far easier to ride than their cumbersome predecessors and they were an instant success. Impressed, the Wrights decided that the bicycle business was worthy of their attention. In 1892, they opened their first cycle shop in Dayton, and they soon prospered; by 1896, the Wright name was well known in the area. Soon, they were manufacturing their Wright Special, an $18 bestseller. At the time, there were about a thousand bicycle manufacturers in the United States, supplying countless bicycle shops, but there was business enough for all. The Wrights did well and might have stayed in the business permanently had it not been for a fatal accident in Germany in August 1896.

A noted glider pilot named Otto Lilienthal died when his glider plunged to earth near Berlin. He had been flying what would now be called a hang glider, maintaining some control over the machine through movements of his body, which was suspended beneath the wings. The American magazine *McClure's* had published an article on Lilienthal two years earlier, and the Wrights probably read about him in that journal. Now he was dead — the most successful glider pilot in the world, a man who had flown more than two thousand times. Soon afterward, a disciple of Lilienthal's, Scotsman Percy Pilcher, was killed when his glider broke up in the air. The brothers' interest in flight flared anew. As was their custom, they consulted the available encyclopedias. They found virtually nothing — hardly surprising, since the very idea of flight was revolutionary and, to most people, vaguely sacrilegious. Although a handful of pioneers talked of powered flight, it seemed to be an impossible dream in the late 1890s, the stuff of boys' adventure fiction. Wasn't it as clear as the nose on J.P. Morgan's face that if the Good Lord had intended people to fly, He would have provided them with wings?

WILLS'S CIGARETTES.

LILIENTHAL GLIDING MACHINE.

The Flying Man

A German civil engineer with an interest in flight, Otto Lilienthal thrilled Europe in the 1890s with his death-defying aeronautical feats. He constructed a series of monoplane and biplane gliders — similar to the hang gliders we know today — and dangled from them in flight, controlling them as best he could by shifting his body to maintain balance. Initially, the athletic German relied on a springboard to launch himself but later he preferred taking off from greater heights, either in Germany's Rhinow Hills or from an artificial hill he constructed near Berlin. The elegant gliders, most made of peeled willow wands with a waxed cotton covering,

achieved distances ranging from three hundred feet to over eight hundred feet during some two thousand flights.

As news of Lilienthal's spectacular flights spread, people from all over Europe came to watch him soar through the air. And published accounts — including the feature in *McClure's* magazine that the Wrights probably read — carried his fame across the Atlantic.

But Lilienthal was not simply a daredevil. In 1889, he published a book, *Birdflight as the Basis for Aviation*, which contained extensive data on his research into the effectiveness of various types of wings. The Wrights would rely heavily on his work during construction of their own gliders. And unlike many of his contemporaries who thought flying would be no more challenging than driving a wagon, Lilienthal understood that man must learn how to fly properly if he hoped to conquer the skies — achieving mastery of both his machine and the mysterious medium that surrounded it.

Unfortunately, Lilienthal's mastery of his own flying machines fell short of the mark and he died tragically in 1896, a day after one of his gliders stalled and crashed. His gallant last words, reputedly uttered to his rescuers when they arrived at his side, were "Sacrifices must be made."

Lilienthal had originally thought that powered flight could be achieved by devising a craft with flapping wings. At the time of his death, he was investigating the use of a small carbonic acid gas (now known as carbon dioxide) engine to transform his gliders into actual flying machines. But for the ill-timed gust that killed him, Lilienthal might well be remembered today as the first true flying man.

The dream of flight had captivated mankind for eons. In the 1400s, that amazing begetter of bright ideas, Leonardo da Vinci, had sketched a mechanism that suggested a combination of kite and drawbridge, offering man a means of operating wings by leg power. Wisely, he didn't put it to the test. In 1507, philosopher and physician John Damian made a pair of wings and confidently launched himself from the wall of Stirling Castle in Scotland. He was lucky to escape with nothing more serious than a broken leg. In the early 1700s, a sixty-two-year-old Frenchman, the Marquis de Bacqueville, attached wing-like appendages to his arms and legs and jumped from a tall building in Paris, intending to flutter across the Seine River. He crashed on a barge, alive but with a considerably reduced interest in flying.

Interestingly, even in those early days, the implications of successful flight struck terror into some hearts. In the seventeenth century, a Jesuit monk named Francesco Lana declared that God would never permit the invention of a flying machine. The reasons seemed obvious to him: "Where is the man who can fail to see that no city would be proof against surprise, when the ship could at any time be steered over its squares, or even over the courtyards of dwelling houses, and brought to earth for the landing of its crew? Iron weights could be hurled to wreck ships at sea, or they could be set on fire by fire-balls and bombs: nor ships alone, but houses, fortresses, and cities could be thus destroyed, with the certainty that the airships could come to no harm, as the missiles would be hurled from a vast height?"

Despite such dire predictions, at least two monks, Oliver of Malmesbury and Brother Cyprian, are believed to have experimented with gliders, the latter reportedly gliding down a mountain in Eastern Europe. Hezarfen Celebi, a seventeenth-century Turk, followed John Damian's example, leaping from a tower on the banks of the Bosphorus — where, according to legend, he landed safely in the marketplace of

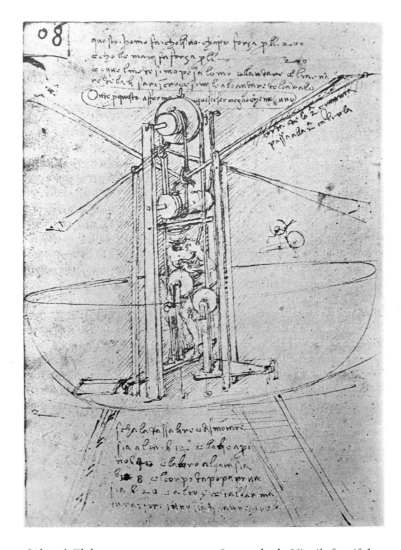

(Above) Elaborate notes accompany Leonardo da Vinci's fanciful fifteenth-century drawing of a man-powered flying machine. (Right) An early sketch by the inventive and eccentric Sir George Cayley, who, by the turn of the eighteenth century, already understood many of the principles of flight.

Scutari. The experience seems to have unnerved him, however, for he kept his feet securely planted on *terra firma* from then on.

Undoubtedly, the most important of the early pioneers was an English baronet named Sir George Cayley, often referred to as the father of aerial navigation. Born in 1773 in Yorkshire, he was a remarkably inventive character who came up with the tension-spoke wheel, the caterpillar tractor, and the hot-air engine. In 1799, while still in his twenties, he engraved one side of a small silver disk with a drawing explaining the effects of the forces of lift, thrust, and drag on a wing. On the reverse side, he sketched an aircraft complete with a fixed wing, a dart-shaped tail, and a pilot in a boat-like compartment with paddles for propulsion. A few years later, he was developing a model glider with wings, a stick-fuselage, and an adjustable tail — an amazingly prescient glance into the future. He even devised control surfaces that hinted at modern elevators and rudders. In 1809, Cayley built a glider large enough to carry a boy. Alas, the name of history's first pilot went unrecorded.

Clément Ader's Eole

Some years later, Cayley's coachman became the first man in the world to complete a flight in a fixed-wing glider. He was fortunate to land safely, whereupon he promptly quit his job the moment he was back on solid ground, protesting that he had been hired to drive, not fly. According to notes in Cayley's hand, the glider weighed 164½ pounds — including 22½ pounds for "sails and yards," two wings totaling 17 pounds, and the "car and working handles and wheels, side masts upright" at 120 pounds. The tail weighed 5 pounds.

Another Englishman, an engineer named William Samuel Henson, had grandiose plans for nothing less than the world's first airline. In the 1840s, he and an associate,

John Stringfellow, designed the ambitious Aerial Steam Carriage which boasted a 150-foot wingspan and was powered by a single steam engine driving a pair of six-bladed pusher propellers. Lacking the funds to develop their aircraft, Henson and Stringfellow became the victims of sharp businessmen attracted to the idea of flying fare-paying passengers all over the world. But the Aerial Transit Company never got off the ground, and neither did the Aerial Steam Carriage — undoubtedly a good thing, for it featured no means of maintaining lateral stability. Disappointed and discouraged, Henson abandoned England for America.

The French contributed a number of important pioneers, including Alphonse Pénaud, who designed a twin-propeller monoplane in 1876 with retractable landing gear, rudder, and elevators. He never built it, although he did complete a number of successful model aircraft powered by lengths of twisted rubber. In fact, the Wrights' toy helicopter was a variation on a Pénaud design. Another Frenchman, Felix du Temple de la Croix, built a machine with a hot-air engine. A sailor was installed as pilot, although he lacked any form of control. The machine, mounted on a slender undercarriage, trundled down a hill near Brest in 1874 and managed a hesitant hop into the air, the first in history. In 1890, a noted electrical engineer, Clément Ader, built a frightening-looking machine suggesting nothing more than a powered bat. It was called the Eole and was powered by a four-cylinder steam engine driving a four-blade tractor propeller. Ader claimed that it flew in 1890; two of his employees witnessed the flight, declaring that the aircraft rose to an altitude of about eight inches during its 150-foot-long trip.

A contemporary of Ader's was American-born Sir Hiram Maxim, who invented the devastatingly successful machine gun bearing his name. In 1894, Maxim produced a gargantuan aircraft with a wingspan exceeding one hundred feet and weighing more than three and a half tons. This monstrosity was powered by a pair of highly efficient steam engines, each generating 180 HP (horsepower). Maxim had developed a complex testing apparatus consisting of two levels of rails: one to direct the craft on its takeoff run, the second to prevent it from soaring away — a sensible precaution, considering the machine would have been quite uncontrollable. Maxim tested his aircraft during the summer of 1894 at Baldwyns Park in Kent, England, shattering the bucolic tranquility of the surroundings when his enormous creation puffed and wheezed into motion. It reached a speed of 42 MPH and even achieved some semblance of flight,

tottering a few inches off the track. At this point, a section of guardrail broke away and hit one of the propellers. End of test. And end of Hiram Maxim's experiments in aviation.

Two years later, a distinguished American engineer by the name of Octave Chanute was conducting a series of experiments with gliders on the sand dunes of Lake Michigan. The French-born Chanute had made his reputation by designing such massive projects as the vast Union Stockyards in Chicago, as well as the first bridge across the Missouri River at Kansas City. Long fascinated by the possibility of manned flight, he had in the early 1890s written a series of articles on the subject for the *Railroad and Engineering Journal.* Soon, he was corresponding with dozens of experimenters in many parts of the world, providing advice and financial assistance where necessary. His articles appeared in book form in 1894 as *Progress in Flying Machines,*

WILLS'S CIGARETTES.

CHANUTE.

(Left) Although Sir Hiram Maxim's cumbersome machine was powered by two steam engines that briefly coaxed it into the air, it lacked all the other elements necessary for sustained flight. (Above) Octave Chanute's inventive design for a biplane glider. (Opposite, left) Octave Chanute. (Opposite, right) Chanute's assistant, Augustus Herring, tests the "double-decker" on the sand dunes by Lake Michigan.

and the volume became essential reading for anyone with aeronautical ambitions.

Chanute designed a biplane glider, adopting a rear-mounted tail for longitudinal stability and incorporating a cambered wing section similar to that pioneered by Lilienthal. Perhaps Chanute's most important contribution to aircraft design was the Pratt truss biplane configuration. Originally patented in 1844 for use on railroad bridges, the truss employed two wings solidly connected by vertical struts carrying compressive loads. Tensile loads were transmitted by crossed diagonal wires joining the struts in both the lateral and the fore-and-aft plane. It was simple and highly efficient and became an essential element in virtually all aircraft until the monoplane took over.

Chanute still hoped to achieve automatic stability and his early experiments combined weight shifting and movable surfaces, with disappointing results. In Lilienthal's gliders, the pilot restored balance by shifting his weight, but the limitations of this system of control were obvious. The addition of an aft horizontal tail was suggested by the experimentation of Alphonse Pénaud. At the time of Chanute's glider experiments, an American pioneer, Samuel Pierpont Langley, seemed the most likely to succeed with a man-carrying aircraft. Langley, the eminent secretary of the Smithsonian Institution and a world-famous astrophysicist, had built a twenty-six-pound scale model of a proposed flying machine — a tandem-winged creation powered by a steam engine delivering a single horsepower. After several disappointing failures, Langley's Aerodrome No. 5, as he called it, flew well. Langley set to work to scale his creation to man-carrying proportions.

Such was the state of the art when the Wright brothers began to take an active interest. In May 1899, Wilbur wrote

to the Smithsonian about his interest in aviation: "I am about to begin a systematic study of the subject in preparation for practical work to which I expect to devote what time I can spare from my regular business. I wish to obtain such papers as the Smithsonian has published on this subject and, if possible, a list of other works in print in the English language. I am an enthusiast, but not a crank in the sense that I have some pet theories as to the proper construction of a flying machine. I wish to avail myself of all that is already known and then if possible add my mite to help on the future worker who will attain final success. . . ."

Richard Rathbun, the assistant secretary of the institution, replied, sending a list of recommended works. A good cross-section of the current thinking on "aerial navigation," the works included writings by several pioneers, including Langley and Chanute, plus several pamphlets from the Smithsonian itself and copies of *The Aeronautical Annual* edited by James Means. Thus, the brothers quickly learned who was doing what — and glimpsed the complexities of the task ahead. If such complexities dismayed the Wrights, they didn't admit it. The difficulties seemed only to stimulate them; it was as if they were happy to be confronted by a challenge worthy of their mettle. All their lives, they had found that if they studied a subject hard enough and long enough, the answers invariably presented themselves.

The Wrights were fortunate to have involved themselves in the bicycle business. It provided them with an adequate living and, more important, it was seasonal — busy in the spring and summer, much slower in the fall, and practically dormant in the winter. Thus, the two men had a good deal of spare time in which to indulge themselves in matters aeronautical. They studied the few books in the local library dealing with flying, later augmenting the knowledge with the books recommended by the Smithsonian. The more they read, the more the brothers became convinced that the field

was wide open; no one had attempted to incorporate any real system of flight control into their creations, apparently expecting them to ride the air like well-behaved hummingbirds and descend gently to earth at the end of each voyage.

Possibly the Wrights saw a parallel between cycling and flying. A two-wheeler is virtually useless until it is in motion. Surely, the same could be said of a flying machine. Until it has speed enough to provide lift, it is nothing more than a somewhat ungainly collection of wood and metal parts, and fabric. About one thing the Wrights were adamant — all control had to be placed firmly in the hands of the pilot. While other experimenters might strive for a fully stable aircraft, the Wrights saw that approach as a blind alley.

As the days wore on, the brothers became ever more aware that they were venturing into unexplored territory. There was no flying art, Wilbur observed, "but only a flying problem." The available data were unreliable. Everything had to be developed almost from scratch — airfoil sections, angles of incidence, dihedral, lift, and drag. . . . In their methodical way, the Wrights noted it all down, every morsel of information, every figure, every sketch. They spent countless hours studying birds, noting in particular the way that buzzards reacted to sudden gusts of wind that almost overturned them by simply twisting their wing tips. But how to make an aircraft do the same thing? Wilbur's idea was to make wings that could be adjusted in flight, the trailing edge of one wing being raised while that of the opposite wing was depressed. But how to accomplish that?

In July of 1899, Wilbur was alone in the shop when someone came in to buy a new inner tube. While the customer took the tube out of the box and examined it, Wilbur picked up the empty box and idly twisted the ends in opposite directions. As he did so, a thought occurred to him. The rectangular box could represent a biplane's wings. As one end curved down, the other curved upward. So why shouldn't a

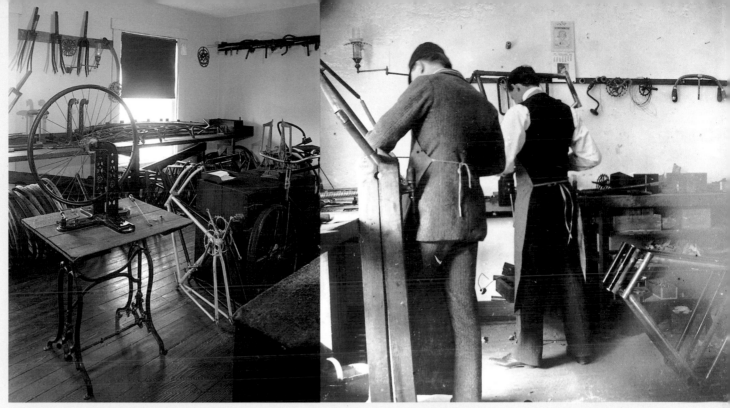

(Opposite, right, and previous page) The Wrights' bicycle shop today. (Far right) Orville, right, and employee Ed Sines at work in the shop in 1897. (Below) The bicycle craze put the world on wheels, giving people a newfound mobility.

The Bicycle Boys

"The flying machine will not be in the same shape or at all in the style of the numerous kinds of cycles, but the study to produce a light, swift machine is likely to lead to an evolution in which wings play a conspicuous part."

— Binghamton *Republican*, July 4, 1896

The bicycle was *the* fad of the 1890s. Attracted by the vehicle's promise of ready and affordable mobility, millions of people flocked to buy them — including large numbers of young women eager to experience a freedom unknown to their mothers. To cash in on the boom, young entrepreneurs all over the United States opened up stores and factories (rather like the dot-com start-ups of the 1990s, but with a higher success ratio).

Given the Wright brothers' technical bent, it's not surprising they got involved with the new machines — selling, repairing, and even building them. And without a doubt, the availability of raw materials, parts, and machinery in their well-equipped shop made a foray into the "flying problem," as Wilbur called it, possible. But the bicycle may have given the brothers more than that. Their experience in dealing with something as inherently unstable as a bicycle gave them a novel approach when it came to the question of how to create a flying machine.

A Dictionary of Flight

By the time the Wrights started their flying experiments, the basic principles of how an airplane worked had been established — thanks to the efforts of earlier pioneers of flight such as George Cayley and Otto Lilienthal.

Lift. This is the very basis of flight. A typical wing or airfoil has a rounded nose or leading edge with a trailing edge that tapers to a thin point. Air passing over the top surface of the wing travels at a greater distance than that passing under it. This creates a difference in pressure, which allows the wing to lift. An airfoil's curvature (the camber) affects its lifting ability and its pitching moment.

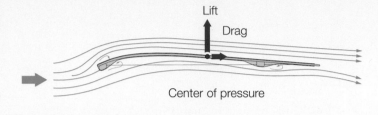

Drag. This is the resistance created by any object immersed in a flow of air. For an airplane to fly, the forward pull (or thrust) must equal or exceed drag. For efficient flight, drag should be as small as possible.

Angle of Incidence. Also called the angle of attack, this is the angle between the chord of the wing and the direction of the relative wind. Lift increases as the angle of incidence increases until stall occurs.

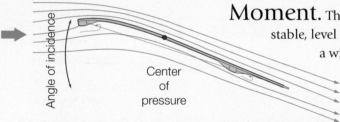

Moment. This is the action on a wing or aircraft that prevents it from remaining in stable, level flight. Since a moment causes rotation, rather than motion in a straight line, a wing on its own tends to dip its nose downward in response to the aerodynamic moment acting on it.

Center of Pressure. The air pressure acts on each little surface area of a wing. The result of all that pressure is a total force called lift, which we can imagine as acting on one spot — the center of pressure. To give their airplanes equilibrium in level flight, many early aviators, the Wrights among them, tried to have the center of pressure coincide with the plane's center of gravity.

Stability. An aircraft that tends always to return to steady flight after a disturbance is said to be stable. The Wrights had some intuitive understanding of stability, but neither they nor their contemporaries knew enough to create a truly stable aircraft. Instead, they contented themselves with unstable, but controllable, machines.

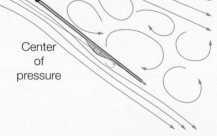

Stall. If the angle of incidence (see above) becomes too large, the air cannot move smoothly over the airfoil, flow separation occurs, the wing loses lift — and the aircraft stalls. The angle at which an aircraft stalls depends on its particular wing. Wilbur was aware that Otto Lilienthal's fateful crash was probably the result of a stall, but only later did he realize that the Wrights' first Flyer was probably often close to stall much of the time.

These basics of flight, while known at the time, were not necessarily well understood. And some — particularly stall and the center of pressure — confounded the brothers throughout much of their career.

biplane's wings be made to twist — or warp — to cope with the conditions aloft, just as the buzzard's did?

It was an exciting idea, a real breakthrough. He could hardly wait to get home and tell Orville about it. That evening, the brothers talked. And talked. Orville quickly became as enthusiastic as Wilbur. No question about it, this changed everything. Now they had to put the idea to the test. They decided to initiate their practical experiments with a kite, just as the English pioneer Cayley had done.

Bubbling with enthusiasm, the Wrights set to work. They built a biplane glider/kite with a five-foot wingspan. Cords were attached to the wing tips so that the kite flyer could control the wing-warping mechanism. Orville was away on a camping trip when Wilbur took the craft to a field just outside Dayton. He found that the wing-warping system worked well, although it was tricky and required practice and patience. Standing on the ground with the cords to his glider/kite, he could soon make the craft swoop and dive like an eagle. It was a thrilling moment. Wilbur was sure he had solved one of the major problems of flight, and he was correct. The Wrights' glider was the world's first flying device capable of being controlled both laterally and longitudinally. The tireless brothers were soon immersed in plans for the construction of a larger glider — in fact, one large enough to carry a man.

The work consumed the winter months. In May 1900, Wilbur decided to write to Octave Chanute. Unsure how his letter would be received by the distinguished engineer, Wilbur went to some lengths to describe the wing-warping

(Above) A modern-day replica of the 1899 kite. The small forward wing — or canard, to use the popular phrase — gave it control in pitch. Cords attached to the wings allowed the operator to control its pitching and rolling motions.

system and the plans for incorporating it in a full-size glider — after which, power would be added. He sought Chanute's advice, remarking that the only way the problems of flight would be solved was through the efforts of many researchers. "The problem is too great for one man alone and unaided to solve in secret." Chanute's reply was useful and encouraging; it was the beginning of a lengthy relationship between him and the brothers from Ohio.

Wilbur had already contacted the U.S. Weather Bureau requesting information on wind conditions in various parts of the country. Strong and steady winds were vital to the Wrights' experiments. The bureau's reply made it clear that it would be necessary to travel a long way from Dayton to find the optimal conditions. The most suitable spot might be Kitty Hawk, a tiny village on the narrow barrier beach off the North Carolina coast not far from Roanoke Island, where English settlers first landed in the 1580s.

Wilbur was soon in correspondence with Joseph Dosher, who headed the Weather Bureau at Kitty Hawk. Dosher responded: "The beach here is about one mile wide, clear of trees or high hills and extends for nearly sixty miles in the same condition. The wind blows mostly from the north and northeast in September and October."

He added a cautionary note: "I am sorry to say you could not rent a house here, so you will have to bring tents." The local postmaster, William J. Tate, a leading light in the small community, also wrote, informing the brothers that they could experiment "on a stretch of sandy land one mile by five with a bare hill in the center eighty feet high, not a tree or bush anywhere to break the evenness of the wind current." While it may have sounded intolerably bleak to most people, to the single-minded Wrights, it sounded like Nirvana. Here, they would have the freedom and space to find the answers to the questions that dominated their every waking moment.

On Thursday evening, September 6, 1900, Wilbur set off by train, an unlikely looking pioneer in his neat suit, stiff collar, and tie. Three days earlier, he had written his father, the bishop, explaining that he was embarking on a vacation combined with learning, adding that he would be "making some experiments with a flying machine." He added that he was taking up the challenge for pleasure rather than profit, although he allowed that there was a "slight possibility of achieving fame and fortune from it. . . ."

Some twenty-four hours later, Wilbur arrived at Old Point Comfort, Virginia, and took passage on the *Pennsylvania* for Norfolk, the former Confederate naval base. He had no time to admire the place, for he had to buy spruce for the glider's

The Three Dimensions of Flight

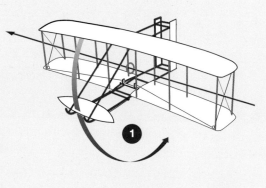

To understand fully what the Wright brothers accomplished — and to grasp how they transferred their understanding of the mechanics of flight to the design of their aircraft — it is necessary to know a little about the movements of an airplane, as well as the terms used to describe them.

1. Pitch.
The movement of the nose of an airplane up or down — as if it were rotating about an axis running through the wing. In modern airplanes, it is controlled by the elevator on the horizontal tail of the aircraft.

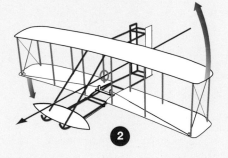

2. Roll.
The rotational movement of an airplane from side to side — around an imaginary axis running the length of the plane. In modern airplanes, it is controlled by the ailerons in the wings.

3. Yaw.
The movement of an airplane's nose from side to side — as if it were rotating about an axis piercing the top of the plane and emerging through the bottom. In modern airplanes, it is controlled by the rudder attached to the vertical tail of the aircraft.

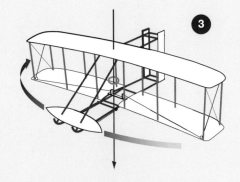

Although the role of these three separate but interrelated movements is understood by all designers and pilots of aircraft today, this was not the case at the turn of the nineteenth century. In fact, with the exception of pitch — which is a fairly straightforward concept — most would-be aviators weren't aware that these were important problems they needed to address if they wanted to fly. The Wright brothers would succeed where so many others had failed because they realized they needed coordinated control over all three of these rotational motions in order to create a practical aircraft.

spars. He found none and had to make do with white pine; he noted in his journal that the cost amounted to $2.70. Adding to his irritation was the fact that the lumber was not available in the sizes he needed. He would have to adjust the plans of the glider when he reached Kitty Hawk, scaling several components to suit the size of the lumber. More delays. More compromise. The temperature approached a hundred degrees, but Wilbur, still wearing his business suit, sweltered without complaint. It would never have occurred to him to slip off his suit jacket and loosen his collar — the Wrights knew the proper way to appear in public, and Wilbur was not about to let a mere heat wave make him compromise his standards.

The trip to the Outer Banks tested Wilbur's resolve, for he had to travel to Elizabeth City and, having just missed the regular Friday boat to Manteo, make his own arrangements for transportation across the forty miles of Albemarle Sound to Kitty Hawk. The trip was made no easier by the fact that he could find no one who had even heard of Kitty Hawk, let alone anyone who could take him there. Wilbur began to feel the dull ache of failure in his gut; soon, he might have to pack up and return to Dayton, having accomplished precisely nothing.

The thought made him renew his efforts. It took him four maddening days but eventually his inquiries led him to Israel Perry, a local river man, a salty, unkempt character who said he knew where Kitty Hawk was and, yes, he would take the gentleman there, along with all his cargo. Relieved, Wilbur checked out of his hotel, expecting Perry's boat to be moored at the town waterfront. He was wrong; it was three miles downriver. The only way to reach the vessel was by water, traveling in a dubious-looking skiff crewed by Perry and a youthful deckhand.

Tight-lipped, apprehensive for both his own safety and that of his precious cargo, Wilbur agreed. He had little choice; no other transport was available. The trip downriver

was a nightmare. The skiff took on water and had to be bailed constantly. Wilbur breathed a sigh of relief when they arrived at Perry's vessel, the *Curlicue*, a flat-bottomed fishing schooner that bobbed on the surface, shifting uneasily with every puff of wind.

Wilbur clambered aboard. Relief turned to horror: "When I mounted the deck of the larger boat, I discovered at a glance that it was in worse condition if possible than the skiff," he later wrote. "The sails were rotten, the ropes badly worn and the rudderpost half rotted off, and the cabin so dirty and vermin-infested that I kept out of it from first to last." Wilbur decided to remain on deck throughout the trip.

It was almost dark when the schooner set sail, slipping into the open waters of the sound, its threadbare sails flapping dispiritedly in the freshening breeze. But within a few minutes, everything changed. The wind suddenly strengthened, churning the black water into angry whitecaps. The schooner skidded on the turbulent surface, its flat bottom making handling almost impossible. Despite the weather, Wilbur remained on deck, hunched against the elements, wondering how long the sorry contraption would survive.

The weather worsened. A full-scale storm hit the area, with thunder and lightning ripping the dark sky. The wind became ferocious, sending waves crashing onto the sagging vessel. Wilbur was drenched, his natty suit now plastered about him, an unwelcome second skin. He and the crew fought to secure the tired old sails. "Why didn't I run at the first sight of this bucket?" Wilbur asked himself.

Israel Perry saved the day. A born sailor — if a casual boatswain — he brought them safely through, docking with aplomb. Wilbur breathed again. He had arrived at the Outer Banks. The trip from Dayton had taken him seven days. After eating a small jar of jelly that his sister Katharine had given him, he took catnaps until the reluctant dawn. It was an inauspicious beginning to an adventure that would change the world.

The Outer BANKS

*"We certainly can't complain of the place. We came down here
for wind and sand, and we have got them."*

— Orville Wright to his sister Katharine, late September, 1900

Sore and stiff after a miserable night on the deck of the *Curlicue*, Wilbur made his way to the residence of William Tate, the local postmaster. Wilbur knew the family, having corresponded with Tate, and he received a warm welcome. Visitors were rare on the Outer Banks, and understandably so. It was desolate here — a strip of windblown sand that followed the mainland coast, a bleak geographical afterthought pummeled daily by powerful winds. Wilbur noted with approval the strength of the wind. The Weather Bureau hadn't led him astray.

The locals intrigued him. They seemed totally unaware of the outside world. He noted in a letter to his father that Tate was an individual of some standing in the minuscule community, living in an above-average house, although by Dayton standards it was primitive — unpainted, lacking carpets, and containing no books or pictures. Unsophisticated the local residents may have been, but Wilbur found them generous and cooperative. When Mrs. Tate learned that Wilbur had eaten nothing but jelly for two days, she immediately whipped up a tasty breakfast of ham and eggs for

him — a veritable feast on the Outer Banks, where eggs were far from plentiful.

"Their yearly income is small. I suppose few of them see two hundred dollars a year," Wilbur wrote. "The ground here is a very fine sand with no admixture of loam that the eye can

(Opposite) A kite soars through the air on the same powerful winds that made the once-remote Outer Banks an ideal testing ground for the Wright glider. (Left) Postmaster William Tate and his family, on the porch of their home at Kitty Hawk, North Carolina.

detect, yet they attempt to raise beans, corn, turnips, &c., on it. Their success is not great but it is a wonder that they can raise anything at all. . . . "

While he waited for Orville to arrive, Wilbur busied himself assembling the glider. As he worked, he redesigned many

(Above) Some of the men from the U.S. Life Saving Station at Kill Devil Hills, North Carolina (below, left), head out to sea. The seven members of the station (below, right) would later be pressed into service by Orville and Wilbur as the world's first aircraft ground crew. This photo was taken by the Wrights shortly after their arrival in the fall of 1900. (Opposite) Once the construction of the 1900 glider was complete, Wilbur and Orville pitched a tent on the dunes.

U.S. LIFE SAVING STATION

components to suit the size of the lumber he had been able to purchase in Norfolk. The high-quality sateen wing covering had to be recut and resewn because the principal components — the wings — were now a different size than had been envisaged, having shrunk from the original span of 19½ feet to 17½ feet. The chord (wing width) was 5 feet. Total cost: $15.

September 28 was a red-letter day. Orville arrived at Kitty Hawk, having enjoyed a much easier trip than his brother. He brought with him supplies of coffee, tea, and sugar, commodities that were virtually unobtainable locally. For a few days, the brothers lodged with the obliging Tates, then they set up camp about half a mile away, their tent roped securely to a tree. The locals watched the proceedings with the wide-eyed fascination of witnesses to some arcane ritual.

In mid-October, strong winds battered the region. The powerful winds were useful, enabling the Wrights to fly the glider/kite with various payloads. Just south of their camp, the brothers set up a triangular derrick about a dozen feet in height. This they planned to use to keep the rope taut during flights, allowing them to become totally familiar with the controls before they attempted manned glider flights — if, indeed, they ever did.

Chanute had expressed his reservations about this approach. "As for myself, I have always felt that restraining ropes were a complication which not only vitiated the results but might lead to accidents from rotation of apparatus or collision with supports, and I have preferred preliminary learning on a sand hill and trying ambitious feats over water. . . ."

In essence, Chanute was saying that the brothers would have to learn the hard way — by flying, making mistakes, and

profiting from those mistakes. The Wrights soon came to agree with him. They had originally calculated that they would need a steady wind of 17 to 20 MPH to support the manned glider — which, in its original form, had a wing area of 195 square feet. Now the wing area was only 175 square feet. With an empty weight of 50 pounds and a pilot weighing 145 pounds,

Camp, 1900, Kitty Hawk.

the wing loading was 1.2 pounds per square foot.

They tested the craft in various configurations: "We tried it with [the] tail in front, behind, and every other way," Orville later noted. Evidently, lack of success had its impact on Wilbur's morale, at least for a while: "When we got through, Wil was so mixed up he couldn't even theorize. It has been with considerable effort that I have succeeded in keeping him in the flying business at all," he reported in a letter home.

Spring scales attached to the restraining ropes enabled the

brothers to make measurements of lift and drag — but these were disappointing. Again and again, the glider's wings produced less lift than the brothers had predicted, based on Lilienthal's data. Three possible explanations presented themselves: 1) the fabric covering was not sufficiently airtight; 2) the camber of their airfoil (1:22) was too shallow for Lilienthal's data to be applicable; or 3) Lilienthal was in error. The Wrights

Orville pulled the craft back to earth. On another occasion, later in the season, the brothers hauled in the craft after a brief flight as a kite. Absorbed in animated conversation, they momentarily turned their attention from the machine — just as nature delivered a fierce gust of wind that picked up the craft, slamming it into the ground amid a heart-stopping cacophony of crackings and splinterings. Stunned, silent,

(Left) A modern replica of the 1900 glider. (Opposite) During the first autumn on the Outer Banks, the Wright brothers flew their glider mostly as a kite (top left). Controlling it was tricky (bottom left). This accident occurred when a gust caught the glider and slammed it into the sand. Once the Wrights returned to Dayton, Mrs. Tate removed the sateen fabric from the abandoned glider to fashion dresses for the Tate girls. (Opposite, right) Young Tom Tate and a prize catch pose in front of the 1900 glider.

favored the second hypothesis. They planned to build their next glider with a more highly cambered airfoil.

Most of the time, the craft was flown as a kite — first from the tower, more often from the ground with handheld ropes. Nevertheless, for a few incredible seconds, both brothers did experience the incomparable sensation of riding on the air, watching the sandy ground drop away — exciting moments, made nerve-jangling by the difficulty of operating the controls. The elements didn't help. On his first venture aloft, Wilbur found the machine bouncing like a bucking bronco. Alarmed,

Wilbur and Orville dragged the wreckage to their tent. Was this the end of their experiments? Both men wrestled with their emotions. Why not just pack up and return to Ohio? Why not admit failure and go back to the bicycle business? At least they understood that — which was more than they could say about flying. Flight was a conundrum buried inside a haystack full of riddles. Just as you unearthed one truth, along came another to contradict it and confound you.

The brothers surveyed the damage, then went to bed, dispirited and disappointed. A good night's sleep worked wonders. In the morning, well rested, they felt better. They wouldn't let this setback deter them. No doubt, they would be confronted by many more before their work was done. They decided to develop several variations on the basic design: with the elevator (which they called the rudder) in front, then in the rear; loaded with up to seventy-five pounds of chains, and empty. The aircraft was flown mostly as a kite, and the results

were diligently noted. When the performance failed to meet their expectations, they wondered whether they were achieving anything worthwhile. Did all those numbers they kept jotting down have any real significance? Were they building an important library of knowledge, or was it all a monstrous waste of time? They weren't sure, but they were achieving a certain familiarity with the air, the invisible mantle surrounding the earth, with all its moods and tempers. Bit by bit, they found that they were able to react instinctively as they steered the craft about the North Carolina sky. The operator — pilot

or rope handler — could never relax, for the air was seldom perfectly calm. And on those rare occasions when it did settle down, the craft itself seemed to acquire the urge to wander off to the right or left, or up or down. Flying demanded your ceaseless devotion, your total commitment. The brothers moved to Big Kill Devil Hill, four miles away from their camp — a sizable hillock whose northeast slope faced the prevailing winds.

Another individual is said to have taken to the air that year. Ten-year-old, seventy-pound Tom Tate, Bill's nephew, claimed to have flown in the kite version of the Wright machine, although the Wrights made no mention of the flight in their journals. Orville said of Tom that he could "tell more big yarns than any kid of his size I ever saw," so doubt exists as to the veracity of his claim.

The 1900 flying season was short; the Wrights spent less than a month at Kitty Hawk. Nevertheless, they were reasonably pleased with their progress as they headed back to Dayton in the latter part of October. They had accumulated about three minutes of free flight, each brother having experienced a few seconds in control. The rest of the time had been spent in pilotless trials. Orville and Wilbur had spent less time in the air than Lilienthal, but they were convinced that they understood more than the unlucky German ever did. Yet there was still so much to discover — and they kept on studying birds, noting such facts as the efficiency with which certain creatures coped with fierce winds; how birds rarely attempted to soar in damp conditions; how they could not soar to leeward of a descending slope unless at a great height. Unfortunately, the observations were largely a waste of time, for there seemed to be little in bird flight to help solve the mystery of manned flight. Orville later wrote: "Learning the secret of flight from a bird was a good deal like learning the secret of magic from a magician. After you know the trick and what to look for, you can see things you didn't notice when you did not know exactly what to look for."

Back in Ohio, the Wrights reviewed their experiences on the Outer Banks. Wilbur wrote to Chanute, summarizing their findings: "At first, the machine was curved laterally to obtain the effect of dihedral angles, but we found the effect very unsatisfactory in gusty winds. Control was much easier after we made it straight. . . . We soon found that our arrangements for working the front rudder and twisting the planes were such that it was very difficult to operate them simultaneously." (Again, Wilbur's reference to the rudder is what today we would call an elevator.)

Chanute had been asked to prepare an article for a technical journal of the day. He wrote to Wilbur, asking permission "to allude to your experiments in such [a] brief and guarded way as you may indicate." Wilbur's response gave a hint of the caution that was beginning to influence the Wrights. He told Chanute that he had no objection to the principle of wing warping being mentioned in the forthcoming article, but he was adamant that no structural details be provided. In other words, Chanute could relate what had been accomplished, as long as he didn't say how. At the time it seemed a reasonable attitude, but it would eventually lead to endless litigation and many challenges to the Wright brothers' claim that they were the first to fly a heavier-than-air machine. The 1900 flight season had been a short one, but it had served to "confirm the correctness of our original opinions."

Why was wing warping so important?

Wing warping lies at the heart of the Wright brothers' triumph. Yet its significance is not immediately apparent. What did wing warping do? And what difference did it make in flight?

In the gliders and early planes the Wrights designed, the pilot shifted the cradle he lay in so that the trailing edges of the wings on one side of the plane were bent down, while the edges of the wings on the opposite side of the plane moved up. This created a difference in the angle of incidence — and, hence, the lift — on the two sides of the plane. In other words, one side moved up, the other side moved down, and the difference in lift caused the aircraft to roll. When the wings were warped in the opposite direction, the plane returned to its original position.

By contrast, Cayley, Lilienthal, and other early pioneers of flight sought to make their craft inherently stable in roll. Cayley had figured out how to do this by incorporating "dihedral" — creating wings with a shallow upward vee shape. According to their thinking, when a wing having dihedral rolled and started to slide to one side — or was struck by a gust from the side — the opposing wings were exposed to slightly different angles of incidence and therefore had slightly different lift. That difference in lift caused the plane to roll back to its original position.

But Wilbur had noticed something about the flight of birds — they didn't depend on "passive" stability. A buzzard caught by a gust of wind would twist its wings to alter their relative lift in order to restore itself to level flight. (In fact, although Wilbur was not aware of it, wing warping as a means of providing active stability and control in roll was discovered first by aviation pioneer John J. Montgomery in the early 1880s. Like Wilbur, Montgomery learned from the birds. He then constructed a series of gliders incorporating wing warping.)

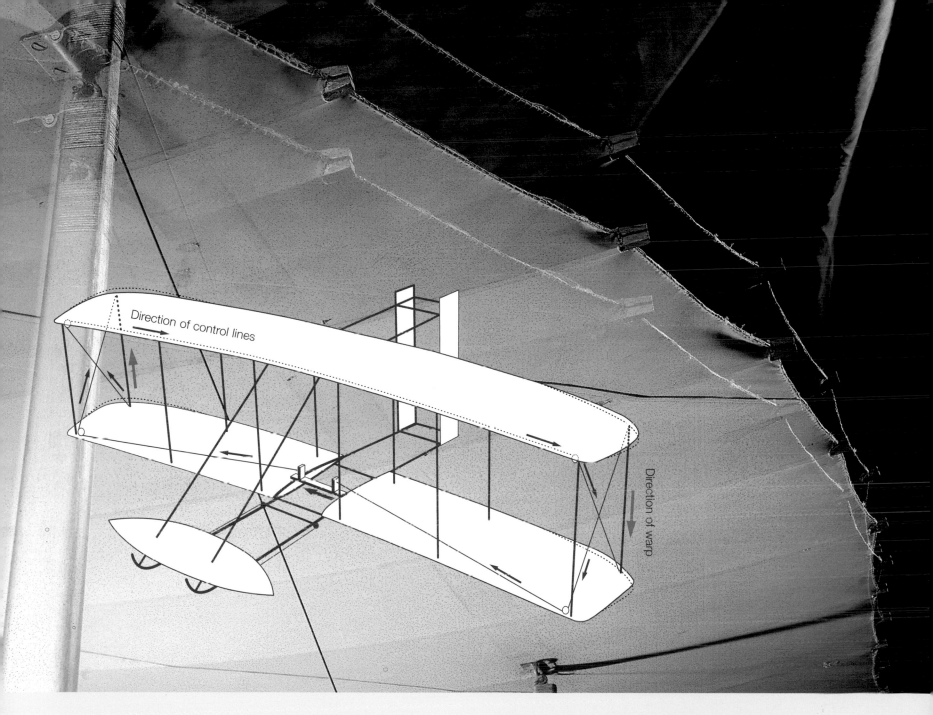

Direction of control lines

Direction of warp

The Wrights realized that wing warping gave the pilot active control over his plane's lateral movements. But it also played another critical role in flight maneuvering. Cayley and many of the Wrights' contemporaries assumed that a plane would be turned like a ship — via the rudder. But this didn't work well, since the airplane skidded crudely. Wilbur determined that the way to turn an aircraft was by rolling into the turn. In other words, the pilot would warp the wings, the plane would roll, and then it would bank into the turn.

Although Wilbur may well have observed birds executing a similar maneuver, it was actually the mechanics of bicycling that inspired him this time. On a bicycle, he recalled, the cyclist turned using the handlebars — but he also leaned over, rolling slightly into the curve, which made for a tighter, more elegant turn. Today, although planes no longer literally warp their wings, the modern equivalent — ailerons — does the same job.

A New GLIDER

"After almost numberless small changes we think our machine will now give results within 2 or 3 percent of the real truth. . . ."

— Wilbur Wright to Octave Chanute, November 22, 1901

Wilbur and Orville spent the winter calculating and recalculating, checking and rechecking their figures, formulating their plans for the 1901 glider. They debated every step — one brother taking a position, the other taking the opposing view. Then casually, almost unthinkingly, they would switch positions and argue the point anew. The rapport between the two men was almost supernatural.

The work went well. The new glider would closely resemble the earlier craft, but would embody a number of very important advances. It was larger, having a wingspan of twenty-two feet and a wing area of about three hundred square feet — making it the largest glider anyone had attempted to fly. The total weight of the structure was now ninety-eight pounds; the wing loading, with pilot, was 0.84 pounds per square foot — a reduction of nearly one-third. The other major modification was the increase in the camber of the wings, from 1:22 to 1:12.

The brothers retained the forward elevator. They trusted it, believing that it had already prevented serious crashes that would otherwise have occurred because of stalling, when their air speed had dropped off until it was no longer sufficient to keep them aloft. A frightening condition — and the one, they were convinced, that had killed Lilienthal. To their considerable relief, the Wrights had discovered that when the flying speed dropped to the point where the air could no longer support the craft, the forward elevator enabled the craft to sink to the ground in a level position, landing back on the earth with nothing more than a thump.

The forward elevator also provided a visual indicator of the craft's attitude in flight. Years later, Orville wrote: "We originally put the elevator in front at a negative angle to provide a system of inherent stability which it would have furnished had the center of pressure on curved surfaces traveled forward, as was supposed, instead of backward with increase in the angle of attack. . . . We retained the elevator in front for many years because it absolutely prevented a nose dive such as that in which Lilienthal and many others since have met their deaths." (In fact, the front-mounted elevator actually aggravated the craft's instability. Had the Wrights been better informed about the flight characteristics of various airfoils, they would undoubtedly have developed a different configuration — as they did in later years. The comforting "mushing" of the first Wright gliders was caused by their center of gravity being located so far back, not by the "canard" tail configuration.)

On July 7, 1901, the brothers set off again for the Carolina coast, establishing a new camp at Kill Devil Hills, near Kitty Hawk. It consisted of a large tent for the men and a wooden shed for the glider. They were pleased with what they had done. "The building is a grand institution," Orville wrote his sister Katharine, "with awnings at both ends; that is, with big doors hinged at the top, which we swing open and prop up, making an awning the full length of the building at end. We keep both ends open almost all the time and let the breezes have full sway."

Orville's enthusiasm was short-lived. A new and utterly wanton foe laid siege to the camp: billions of mosquitoes, the hungriest of their kind. The pests arrived at the same time as Edward C. Huffaker, an associate of Octave Chanute's, who had come to Kitty Hawk to witness the Wrights' experiments

(Above) Orville poses proudly beside the 1901 glider, with its twenty-two-foot wingspan. (Below) The new campsite at Kill Devil Hills. (Pages 42–43) With Wilbur at the controls, Bill and Dan Tate let the wind lift the redesigned glider off the top of the dunes.

— and who quickly made himself thoroughly unpopular with the brothers, thanks to his tedious moralizing and his reluctance to do any real work. However, the irritation he caused was nothing compared with that of the mosquitoes. The battle with the insects "was the beginning of the most miserable existence I ever passed through," Orville declared. "They chewed us clear through our underwear and socks. Lumps began swelling up all over my body like hens' eggs."

Desperate, the men resorted to escaping to bed at about five in the afternoon. "We put out cots under the awnings and wrapped up in our blankets, with only our noses protruding from the folds, thus exposing the least possible surface to attack. Alas! Here nature's complicity in the conspiracy against us became evident. The wind, which until now had been blowing over twenty miles an hour, dropped off entirely. Our blankets then became unbearable. The perspiration would roll off us in torrents. We would partly uncover and the mosquitoes would swoop down upon us in vast multitudes."

The following night, the men attempted to protect themselves with mosquito nets. The insects promptly ate through them. The only solution was to burn old tree stumps, producing so much smoke that the mosquitoes buzzed away,

defeated. But the remedy was as unpleasant as the problem. The men could hardly breathe in the roiling smoke. Another of Chanute's protégés, a young physician/aviation enthusiast named George A. Spratt, arrived. In the morning, he said he had never endured such a night.

Eventually, mercifully, the mosquitoes went on their way. The men dragged the glider out to Big Hill. Their enthusiasm disappeared as rapidly as the retreating mosquitoes. "Our first experiments were rather disappointing," Orville wrote. "The machine refused to act like our machine last year and at times seemed to be entirely beyond our control."

The new craft was flown both as a glider (with Wilbur at the controls) and as a kite. It demonstrated a dismaying affection for solid ground, flopping back to earth moments after each launch. The Wrights tried to reason their way out of the dilemma. Where had they gone wrong? Had they placed the pilot's position too far forward? It seemed possible that the weight of the pilot might be dragging the aircraft down.

The sweating team heaved the glider up Big Hill again and again. Not until the ninth attempt did they achieve a satisfactory performance. At first, the glider seemed uncertain, skimming low over the sandy ground; then, to the men's delight, it climbed, and completed a flight of some three hundred feet. Although relieved, the Wrights were still

The gliders were always tested as kites (opposite, far left) before Wilbur attempted a free glide (left). (Right) The brothers constructed a more utilitarian structure in the summer of 1901. Each end opened out to allow easy removal of the glider and also provided welcome shade from the scorching sun. Seated from left to right are Octave Chanute, Orville, and Edward Huffaker. Wilbur is standing.

uneasy about the glider's performance. Further tests revealed a tendency to dive or climb so abruptly that it took the utmost skill on the part of the pilot to bring it safely to earth. Gliding was becoming an exercise in violent movements of the elevator control as the glider alternated between swoopings and soarings, like something demented. Although the Wrights had so far avoided disaster, it was clear that they ran a danger of flying into the ground or stalling catastrophically.

Something was seriously wrong with the wings, the brothers surmised, and they set to work to improve the leading edges and reduce the camber of the canard. They scaled the surface area from eighteen square feet to ten. In their tests, they thought they had discovered a fundamental property of airfoils: that camber causes the motion of the center of lift to reverse as the angle of incidence is changed. They concluded that the solution was clear — reduce the camber of the wings. The Wrights reverted to the camber of the 1900 glider by installing king posts on the lower wing and rigging truss wires to pull the middle sections of the ribs downward. The benefits were immediate. Wilbur made some thirty flights, the longest being of 17.5 seconds' duration, during which he covered a distance of 390 feet. (The problem had been fixed, but not for the reason they suspected.)

When Chanute visited the camp in early August, he was vastly impressed by the Wrights' progress. Straight and level glides were by now commonplace. Wilbur's skill enabled him to follow every hillock and hump. Chanute was captivated. The brothers from Ohio seemed to have conquered the air. The brothers themselves knew better. They still had to unravel the mystery of turning.

So far, Wilbur's attempts to turn had met with limited success. When he'd dip one wing to commence the turn, he would detect a trembling as the lower wing slowed and the higher wing threatened to pull the aircraft into a gyration that future aviators would describe as a spin. It happened to Wilbur on one occasion; fortunately, he was only shaken, but both brothers recognized how close they had come to disaster.

Toward the end of the 1901 flight program, Wilbur began to analyze the behavior of the aircraft in turns. In his diary, he observed that the "upturned wing seems to fall behind, but at first rises." It was all very puzzling. He wrote to Chanute. "The last week was without very great results though we proved that our machine does not turn (i.e., circle) toward the lowest wing under all circumstances, a very unlooked-for result and one which completely upsets our theories as to the causes which produce the turning to right and left."

Practicing turns, Wilbur discovered what is now called adverse yaw. Although the lift on the raised wing is initially greater than that on the lowered wing, so is the drag. The different drag forces tend to turn the aircraft in the direction opposite to the one intended when the rolling motion is initiated. Wilbur's experiments led to the installation of a vertical tail on the next glider. Within three weeks, Wilbur — the theorist, the inventor, the builder, and the test pilot — had made two crucial discoveries that would have an enormous impact on the development of the airplane.

In late August, the brothers headed back to Dayton, simultaneously elated and depressed. They had made progress, but an Everest of problems still bedeviled them. Again and again, they checked their figures and they came to a shocking conclusion: Lilienthal's data were in error. It was tantamount to questioning the law of gravity.

Wilbur revealed this finding to a meeting of the Western Society of Engineers shortly after returning to Dayton. He also explained their use of a forward surface for control and wing warping, but it's doubtful anyone in the audience understood the significance of what he was saying. Wilbur disliked public speaking and hadn't relished the thought of appearing before an audience of professional engineers. He had taken uncommon pains with his attire, borrowing one of Orville's shirts, collars, and a pair of cuff links — and he had journeyed to the meeting in his brother's overcoat. The audience responded enthusiastically, but some of them must have doubted Wilbur's claim that the highly respected Lilienthal could possibly have been so grossly in error in his calculations.

Nevertheless, Wilbur had the utmost confidence in his claims. He and Orville had developed their own data, diligently conducting experiments. One method they used was to modify one of their bicycles, adding a horizontal wheel fitted directly over the front wheel. To compare the effects of wind on different surfaces, they rode the bicycle with a selection of airfoils mounted on the horizontal wheel. Although crude, the device gave them a starting point from which they developed their wind tunnel.

The tunnel was an invaluable tool. While it was by no means the first in history, it was the first to yield results significant to airplane design. Six feet long, sixteen inches square, the wind tunnel had a glass top through which the brothers could observe their experiments and measure the forces and moments on models of wings and tail surfaces. Wind was provided by a small combustion engine that had originally been built by the brothers to drive a lathe, a drill press, and a saw. A honeycomb device straightened out the wind as it came whirling from the fan. The wing or tail section being tested was mounted at the far end of the tunnel; the amount of movement was an accurate indication of the amount of lift generated by different sections. In addition, the amount of drag could be plotted accurately.

A measure of the brothers' meticulous control of the test conditions was their insistence that they stand in precisely the same spot for every experiment and that no large objects, such as furniture, could be moved. Conditions had to be identical from test to test. Over a period of two months, they tested some two hundred wings, comparing aspect ratios, wing shapes, biplane and monoplane configurations. By the end of the year, they had all the data they would need to design their aircraft for the next ten years. "I believe," Orville later wrote, "we possessed more data on cambered surfaces, a hundred times over, than all of our predecessors put together."

He was undoubtedly correct. Unfortunately, Octave Chanute, with the best of intentions, freely discussed with his engineering colleagues the progress of the brothers' work. In years to come, the Wrights would wish that they had kept their secrets to themselves.

The Wind Tunnel

When the Wright brothers began work in 1900 on the first of their gliders, they relied on research material published by Otto Lilienthal in connection with extensive experiments he had conducted to determine the relative lift and drag that was produced by different airfoils. By plugging his data — along with the value for a constant called Smeaton's coefficient — into an equation, the Wrights could calculate the expected lift for a wing made in the shape of one of his airfoils. By 1901, however, they concluded that Lilienthal's data must be wrong: their gliders were still not producing the lift they had expected. They would have to conduct their own experiments, and for that they needed a wind tunnel.

Refining their knowledge of bicycle-based aerodynamic balance, the brothers created a device linking a flat plate and a small test wing. While Lilienthal's experiments had focused on airfoils of various shapes, the Wrights collected data not only for airfoils but also for wings having different shapes and for struts and other structural components — virtually all the information they would need to design airplanes and propellers for the rest of their aviation careers.

During their wind-tunnel tests, Wilbur also changed his

An inside view of the Wrights' wind tunnel shows the balancing vane the brothers constructed, as well as some scraps of wallpaper on which they recorded their observations.

view of Lilienthal's data. When the brothers used Lilienthal's data to estimate the lift they could expect for their 1900 and 1901 gliders, they assumed the value 0.005 for Smeaton's coefficient — first reported by the man himself in 1754, confirmed by others during the next century and a half, and recommended by Lilienthal. This figure was one number they could be sure of, and they had never suspected it could be wrong. But if the value given was too high, then the predicted lift would also be too high.

And wrong it was. By merging their data from their full-scale gliders with that from the wind tunnel, they arrived at the correct value of Smeaton's coefficient — 0.0033. This explained why the lift on their 1900 and 1901 gliders was less than they had anticipated. Lilienthal's data were correct; it was his value — everyone's value — for Smeaton's coefficient that was wrong. Armed with the correct value, the brothers could develop better wings.

The Wrights were not trained scientists and they had no real interest in pure research for its own sake. Nevertheless, their reasoning, experimental work, and findings — carried out in the traditions of the finest scientific research — are remarkable for the time.

4   A Question of CONTROL

The Wrights' 1902 glider had a span of thirty-two feet and a chord of five feet. The wind-tunnel tests had determined that the long, narrow wing was the most efficient form. The new model was the first to incorporate the hip cradle, which operated the warping mechanism. A separate lever for the pilot's left hand operated the horizontal surfaces. It was a cumbersome arrangement, one that demanded considerable dexterity on the part of the pilot — and it would cause problems later in flight trials. For the moment, however, it was the most advanced system in the world.

A double vertical tail, with a surface area of almost twelve square feet, extended some four feet aft of the wings. The double-fin arrangement was chosen in order to add lift when a sideslip began, compensating for adverse yaw. This rudder was not movable.

In late August, the brothers returned to Kitty Hawk and assembled the new machine. After the first cautious test flights, Orville wrote: "We are convinced that the trouble with the 1901 machine is overcome by the vertical tail."

His confidence was premature. Although the vertical tail surfaces seemed to help in the search for stability, they clearly weren't the complete answer. The glider still behaved sometimes as if scared of what was about to take place, dropping a wing and slipping sideways. It acted as if it were on ice. Was it the pilot's fault? Unfamiliarity with the new controls, perhaps?

The brothers continued their testing until September 23. Then the real troubles began.

It had been just another day on the sand. The glider was flying well, with Orville at the controls. Suddenly, stunningly, it all went wrong, largely because Orville was not totally accustomed to the new controls. When one wing got a little high, he moved the cradle accordingly — but neglected to turn the front rudder (elevator) down. The nose angled upward at an alarming rate.

Wilbur soars from the top of Kill Devil Hills and over the campsite in the 1902 glider. Much larger than the previous year's model, this design featured a twin-rudder configuration that was used for preventing sideslips, rather than for steering.

Watching from below with Dan Tate, Wilbur felt his heart skip a beat. The glider slid off into another of those terrifying sideslips. Nothing Orville did could right it. The glider seemed bent on self-destruction. In a moment, it was sinking helplessly; then it crashed into the sand.

Wilbur and Dan Tate ran, gasping, to the wreck, their imaginations painting gruesome pictures of Orville sprawled in the wreckage, bleeding, terribly injured. Or worse. Instead,

(Above) After repeated problems with the fixed twin rudders during early trials, Orville suggested replacing them with a single movable tail. (Opposite) With this modification in place, Wilbur now had lateral control of the glider and could bank it gracefully into turns.

he was already pulling himself out of the mess when the others arrived. He had emerged without a scratch, although his suit coat had suffered a tiny tear. The forward elevator had taken the brunt of the shock and was severely damaged.

Good news and bad news. Orville was alive and well — but the glider still possessed its deadly habits. The brothers discussed the problem as they set about the task of rebuilding the craft. The job took only a few days. On the morning of September 30, their elder brother Lorin arrived at Kitty Hawk. An enthusiastic spectator, he marveled as his younger brothers floated on air. Frustratingly, they had to confine themselves to straight, level flights, only essaying the gentlest form of turn for fear of encountering the deadly condition again.

They discussed it endlessly, analyzed the craft's behavior, questioned every detail of their design. Eventually, they focused on the vertical tail surfaces, since these were the most recent additions to the glider. They tried eliminating one vertical fin. It seemed to make little difference.

It was another of the maddening problems that had beset them throughout their development work. They spent hours on it, postulating, protesting, asserting, contending. After one marathon session, Orville retired to bed, his head swimming, weary but unable to sleep. Too much coffee, he told himself as he settled down. He arose the next morning, puffy-eyed from lack of sleep but excited by what he had figured out. He explained it all to Wilbur and Lorin.

The sideways sliding motion was a distressing feature of both the 1901 and the 1902 gliders, he said. The addition of the vertical fins seemed to have had no beneficial effect. He offered this explanation. As the fixed vertical fins were struck by the wind on the low side, they added to the turning movement. Without vertical fins, the machine would have yawed about its axis the other way. The answer, he explained, between mouthfuls of breakfast, was to make the rudder movable. Thus, as the pilot banked, he could apply pressure to compensate for this dangerous pivoting tendency.

Lorin later said that he had fully expected Wilbur to disagree. It was the standard operating procedure the two brothers had so that they could battle out every last detail. Instead, Wilbur nodded in a deliberate, analytical way as he absorbed what Orville had described. Expecting an argument, Orville got a nod. Wilbur liked his solution. It could well be the answer to their problem. But why burden the pilot with yet another control? Since the pilot would invariably have to operate the rudder whenever he banked, why

"We have far beaten all records for flatness of glides. ..."
— Wilbur Wright to his father, October 2, 1902

(Opposite) Wilbur and Dan Tate fly the 1902 glider as a kite. (Inset) Replicas of the Wrights' 1899 kite and 1902 single-rudder glider show how profoundly the brothers' designs had advanced. (Above) Although Octave Chanute flew his triplane as a kite, he and his assistants had little success with it as a glider.

not combine the controls? Thus, when a pilot entered a turn, the rudder would turn automatically.

They could hardly wait to get to the workshop and start the latest modifications. Quickly, they removed the glider's two vertical fins and replaced them with a single rudder measuring five feet by fourteen inches. By the evening of October 6, the new glider was ready. In the meantime, Octave Chanute had returned with his assistant Augustus Herring and a new, multi-wing glider. The Wrights' welcome must have been a little tight-lipped; they were, after all, fully engaged in their own experiments and didn't have time to entertain others. But the young men had been brought up well — and dear old Chanute had been so helpful in the early days. They made the newcomers as comfortable as they could.

By this time, both brothers were becoming more skilled at flying the glider, maneuvering with growing confidence. In contrast, Chanute and Herring had a terrible time with their craft. The cumbersome multi-wing contraption refused to do more than flop dispiritedly from one launch to another. On October 11, Orville wrote in his journal: "Mr. Herring has decided that it is useless to make further experiments with the multi-wing." He added: "I think that a great deal of the trouble with it came from its structural weakness, as I noticed that in winds which were not even enough for support, the surfaces were badly distorted, twisting so that, while the wind at one end was on the under side, often at the other extreme it was on top. Mr. Chanute seems much disappointed in the way it works."

Over the last few weeks of October, the Wrights made approximately one thousand flights. One flight lasted twenty-six seconds, and several covered more than six hundred feet. Every day brought them more familiarity with their control system; by the end of the month, they had become skilled pilots, able to handle almost any conditions.

It was time for them to think seriously about adding power to their aircraft.

The POWER of Two

"We are thinking of building a machine next year with 500 sq.ft. surface. . . .
If all goes well the next step will be to apply a motor."

— Wilbur Wright to George Spratt, December 29, 1902

Wilbur and Orville discussed it all the way back to Dayton. Their doubts had vanished like a puff of smoke in an Outer Banks blow. They had the aircraft; it flew well and was fully controllable. And, they believed, they had forged ahead of the rest of the world with their research. Incredible. But true.

Now it was time to think about protecting what they had created. Too many people were becoming aware of the Wright brothers and their successes, and there was a very real danger that other aviators might "borrow" their ideas. Already, a French army officer by the name of Ferdinand Ferber was experimenting with gliders based on the Wrights' design. He had corresponded with Chanute, who had sent him a copy of Wilbur's Chicago lecture of September 1901. Now, the Wrights were becoming well known among the small community of aeronautical experimenters. Samuel Langley had written to the Wrights, requesting information about their "special curved surfaces" and their system of control. Were there others waiting in the wings (so to speak), eager to profit from what the Wrights had accomplished?

As soon as the brothers arrived back in Dayton, they started the search for a suitable gasoline engine to power their aircraft. They wrote to a dozen of the companies that comprised the nascent automobile industry. The replies weren't encouraging. All existing engines seemed to weigh too much and to deliver too little power. No one had built the kind of engine the Wrights wanted — and there's little doubt the automakers were wary of becoming involved with "crackpot" aviation projects.

Characteristically, the Wrights decided to build their own engine. Fortunately, they had a highly talented young mechanic named Charles E. Taylor working in their bicycle shop. He later wrote: "The first thing we did as an experiment was to construct a sort of skeleton model in order that we might watch the functioning of the various vital parts before venturing with anything more substantial. Orv and Wil were pretty thorough that way — they wouldn't take anything for granted but worked everything out to a practical solution without too much haste. I think this had a lot to do with their later success.

"When we had the skeleton motor set up, we hooked it up to our shop power, smeared the cylinder with a paint brush dipped in oil, and watched the various parts in action." He added: "It looked good so we went ahead immediately with the construction of a four-cylinder engine. I cut the crankshaft from a solid block of steel weighing over a hundred pounds. When finished, it weighed about nineteen pounds. We didn't have spark plugs but used the old 'make and break' system of ignition [in which the spark is produced by the opening and closing of contact points inside the combustion chamber]. The

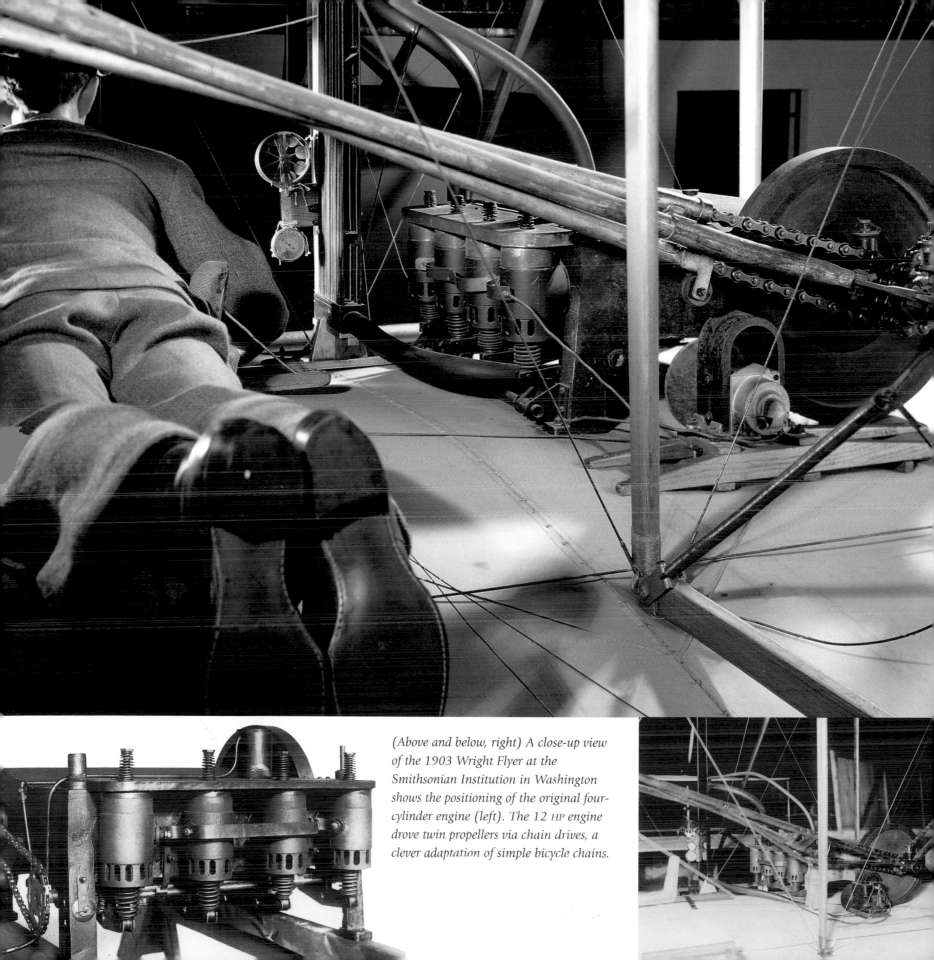

(Above and below, right) A close-up view of the 1903 Wright Flyer at the Smithsonian Institution in Washington shows the positioning of the original four-cylinder engine (left). The 12 HP engine drove twin propellers via chain drives, a clever adaptation of simple bicycle chains.

gas pump was geared on to the camshaft and the gas was led in and made to spread over the chamber above the heated water jackets and this immediately vaporized it. . . ."

It was an elemental kind of engine. But it worked — after a few early glitches. In February 1903, Wilbur and Orville took the engine into the shop for a test run. A flop. The bearings froze, cracking the crankcase. A new casting was ordered immediately, and by May the engine was running satisfactorily.

The brothers were all too conscious of the need for urgency. Langley was having a new engine built in Washington for the Aerodrome, financed by the U.S. military. The Wrights had heard only fragmentary reports about Langley and his aircraft, but they recognized him as a serious competitor, one who might well overtake them in the quest to be the first to fly.

At the same time, the brothers had been busy on their airframe, extending the wingspan to forty feet, four inches, and its chord to six feet, six inches. The new machine would be the largest they had ever constructed, incorporating wing ribs made out of long, thin strips with the lengthy spars sandwiched in between to save weight. In their meticulous way, they even conducted wind-tunnel experiments on the struts between the wings in order to reduce wind resistance to an absolute minimum.

They anticipated little difficulty in designing propellers for their aircraft. After all, propellers had been used to drive ships for eons — and balloons since the mid-1800s, when Henri Giffard completed the first controlled powered flight in history. He had used a three-bladed propeller and managed an airspeed of about 5 MPH. But when the Wrights began to look into available propellers, they were shocked. No one had done any research on the subject, and no one had any advice to offer. Charlie Taylor recalled: "I think the hardest job Wil and Orv had was with the propellers. I don't

believe they were ever given enough credit for that development. They had read up on all that was published about boat propellers, but they couldn't find any formula for what they needed. So they had to develop their own."

Marine propellers had evolved largely through a process of trial and error. Engineers simply experimented with sizes and types of propeller until they found one that met their requirements. The Wrights theorized that an aerial propeller was, in essence, an airplane wing — and, like a wing, it creates a difference in pressure: more on the back of the blade than on the front, just as a wing creates less pressure on the top of the wing than on the bottom. Orville later wrote: ". . . nothing about a propeller, or the medium in which it acts, stands still for a moment. The thrust depends upon the speed and the angle at which the blade strikes the air; the angle at which the blade strikes the air depends upon the speed at which the propeller is turning, the speed the machine is traveling forward, and the speed at which the air is slipping backward; the slip of the air backward depends upon the thrust exerted by the propeller, and the amount of air acted upon. When any of these changes, it changes all the rest, as they are all interdependent upon one another."

Where others attached propellers to their creations and hoped for the best, the Wrights set out to match up propeller and machine to a degree never before attempted — yet another reason why there is no foundation to the persistent myth that the Wrights were a couple of ill-educated bicycle mechanics who stumbled upon the secret of flight. What they achieved in the design of the propellers alone was extraordinary. And it was the result not of happenstance but of unremitting labor. Every day, they worked. And argued. Over every detail.

Taylor wrote: "Both the boys had tempers, but no matter how angry they ever got, I never heard them use a profane

The design of the 1903 Wright Flyer featured a narrow wing composed of lightweight ribs, with the lengthy spars sandwiched in between to save weight. The replica (opposite) was built by author Fred Culick and members of the Wright Flyer Project.

word. . . . The boys were working out a lot of theory in those days and occasionally they would get into terrific arguments. They'd shout at each other something terrible. I don't think they really got mad, but they sure got awfully hot.

"One morning, following the worst argument I ever heard, Orv came in and said he guessed he'd been wrong and they ought to do it Wil's way. A few minutes later, Wil came in and said he'd been thinking it over and perhaps Orv was right." Eventually the two brothers began to re-argue the case, this time each taking the other's original position!

Just how far ahead of the pack were the Wrights? One indication is the fact that years later, after the successful 1903 flights at Kitty Hawk, leading French aviators such as Henri Farman, Henri Voisin, Ferdinand Ferber, and Léon Delagrange were still using empirical methods to select the best propellers for their aircraft. No other designers even attempted to emulate the Wrights' scientific methods.

Bearing in mind the machine's height above the ground, Orville and Wilbur selected propellers eight feet, six inches in diameter, calculating that they could push a greater mass of air with two propellers rotating slowly than they could with one propeller spinning rapidly. It's especially interesting to note that they designed the two propellers to be contra-rotating — that is, turning toward one another — to eliminate torque. This remarkably advanced idea would not be redis-covered until the late 1930s, when such modern aircraft as the Lockheed P-38 fighter appeared. The Wrights' research enabled them to predict propeller performance with astonishing accuracy.

The brothers made their first propeller with a hatchet and a draw knife, carving a helicoidal twist into a solid block of wood. They tested the propeller on a 2 HP motor behind the bicycle shop. So far, so good. Now, they proceeded to design the actual propellers for the aircraft. They would be made of three laminations of spruce, their tips covered with a thin layer of light duck canvas for reinforcement.

Years later, more accurate tests determined that their propellers had a greater than seventy-percent efficiency. In other words, two-thirds of the 12 HP reaching the propellers was converted to thrust, almost exactly what the Wrights had calculated.

These were exciting times. The Wrights had solved most of the major problems concerned with powered flight. It only remained for them to apply the fruits of their labors to the full-size machine.

Wilbur was adamant that not a word be said about it publicly. Speaking at another meeting of the Western Society of Engineers, he impressed his listeners with details of the 1902 experiments, while he raised a few eyebrows with his criticism of the work of Maxim and Langley. Wilbur didn't care. He knew, even if his audience didn't, that his criticisms were well founded. He had the figures to prove it.

Interest in the brothers' experiments mounted among the small coterie of aerial pioneers in the United States and abroad. Octave Chanute kept asking the brothers if this acquaintance or that might travel to Kill Devil Hills to check on their progress. Particularly irritating was the possibility that Augustus Herring might show up; he had made himself a notable nuisance the previous year. Another individual they preferred not to see was the excitable French army officer Ferdinand Ferber, who wanted to buy Wright gliders. The Wrights had more important work to do.

On Wednesday, September 23, 1903, they left Dayton for Elizabeth City.

Without access to the work of other engineers or scientists, Orville and Wilbur fashioned highly effective propellers for their aircraft. They realized that they needed to treat the propeller as if it were a wing in motion, subject to the same aerodynamic forces. (Opposite) This triumph of grace and technology is captured in Dan Patterson's dramatic photograph of the 1905 Flyer's massive propellers.

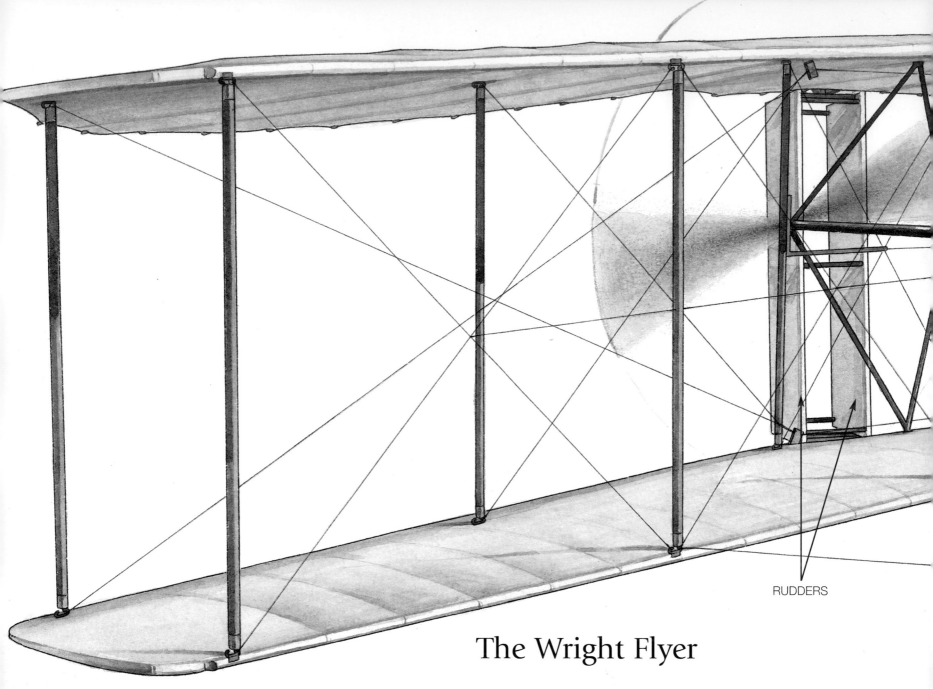

RUDDERS

The Wright Flyer

With its engine, propellers, and massive ribbed wings, the aircraft the Wrights designed in 1903 was a startling advance beyond their gliders. And not merely because it was powered. The Flyer was almost five hundred pounds heavier than the glider, and the wing loading per square foot had more than doubled. With its weight and size, this new flying machine could no longer be launched from the top of a hill — it would need a track and a good distance to get airborne. The brothers were methodical workmen and they had mastered the mechanics of flight. The design of the Flyer was a testament to that. Still, they must have looked on their creation with some trepidation. Unlike today's test pilots, the Wrights didn't have the luxury of high-speed taxi tests and tentative hops off the ground to gain acquaintance with their machine's handling qualities. Their first trials with the propellers running would be attempts to take off and fly.

The 1903 Flyer is preserved today at the National Air and Space Museum in Washington. (Opposite, left) The plane featured twin forward elevators to control pitch. (Opposite, right) The engine, the radiator, and the distinctive droop (anhedral) of the wings are evident here.

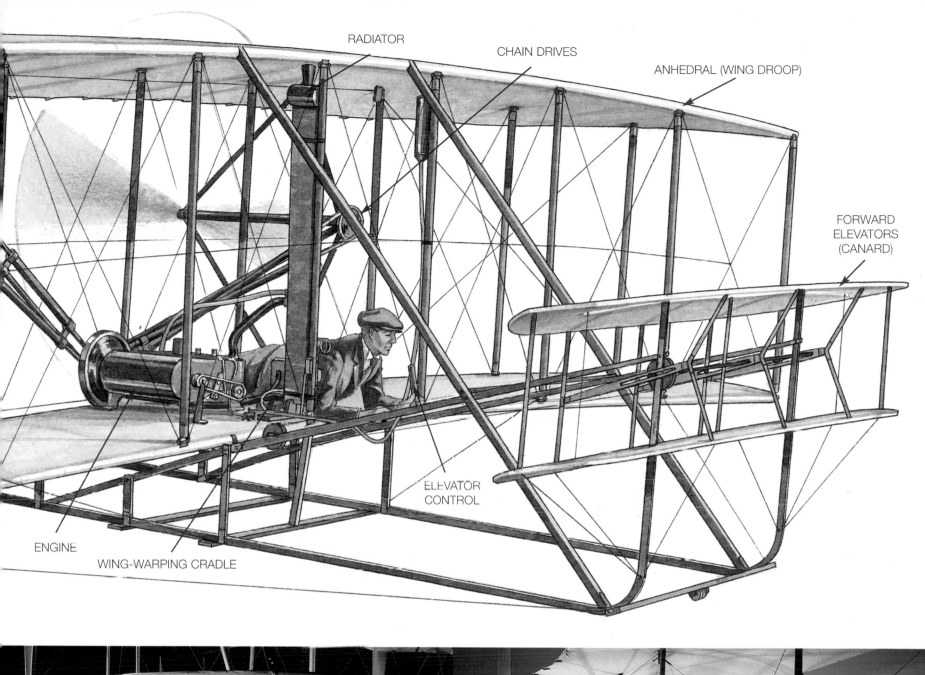

RADIATOR

CHAIN DRIVES

ANHEDRAL (WING DROOP)

FORWARD
ELEVATORS
(CANARD)

ELEVATOR
CONTROL

ENGINE

WING-WARPING CRADLE

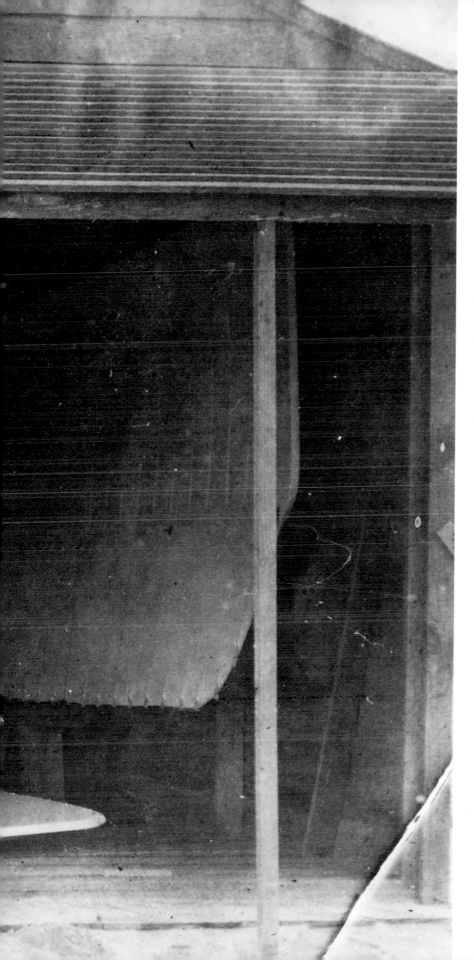

TESTING 6
Time

During the long journey to the East Coast, the brothers went over every detail of their aircraft. They had the utmost confidence in their calculations; they had built the aircraft themselves and had no doubt of its ability to fly.

The outlook was rosy, but for the existence of Samuel Langley, the secretary of the Smithsonian, who, according to reports, was nearly ready to test his aircraft, the cumbrous Aerodrome. It would be piloted by an engineer, twenty-two-year-old Charles Manly, who had done a good job of modifying a rotary engine built by the New York firm of Stephen M. Balzer to provide the necessary power. But incredibly, Manly had no piloting experience, not even on gliders. He apparently intended to pick up the necessary skills in flight.

How did the Aerodrome compare to the Wright Flyer? The brothers believed their design was far superior to Langley's, which had been built for the military at a vast expenditure of public funds — more than $50,000 — compared with a few hundred dollars of the Wrights' money for the Flyer. The most important question: Which aircraft would be first to take to the air under its own power?

The brothers arrived at Kill Devil Hills on August 28 and

When the Wrights returned to Kill Devil Hills in August 1903, the buildings were remarkably intact, despite a year of particularly violent weather. (Opposite) Orville, in front, works at assembling the latest Flyer. (Insets) The reconstructed plane shed and living quarters today.

Although the living quarters (left) at Kill Devil Hills were modest, the kitchen (above) was well stocked with provisions. A chair near the stove (below) and the bunks under the eaves (bottom) provided some comforts at the end of a long day on the windy dunes.

found, much to their relief, that things seemed to be in good order — except that the wooden shed was several feet nearer the ocean than when they had left the previous year. Dan Tate reported that the weather had been notably violent during their absence, with vicious storms and lightning "so terrible that it turned night into day," as Orville wrote to Katharine. The 1902 glider was undamaged. "We will have the old machine ready for practice on days of good winds, and will work on the new machine on rainy and calm days," he added. "The hills are in the best shape for gliding they have ever been, and things are starting off more favorably than in any year before."

The Wrights began their new season by attempting to hover in their glider, as they had seen the buzzards and hawks do with ease. Using the full range of controls they now possessed, they found themselves able to hang almost motionless in the air. Orville set the record at one minute, eleven and four-fifths seconds. (Not until 1911 was that record broken — and the man who broke it was Orville Wright.)

In mid-October, while they worked on the new machine, they heard about Langley's first attempt at manned flight. Perched on a catapult atop a houseboat, the ill-proportioned aircraft traveled briskly along the track — then dived straight into the water. The pilot, Manly, managed to scramble clear of the wreckage. The newspapers had a field day at Langley's expense, one saying that the machine flew like "a handful of mortar" and bewailing the monstrous waste of public money.

Luckily, the Wrights had no newspaper reporters to worry about as they conducted their experiments. The area was so bleak, so uninviting, that they were able to prepare their aircraft without interruption. But when they installed the engine that Charlie Taylor had designed and built, they discovered the machine weighed in at a formidable 605 pounds, not counting the pilot — some 70 pounds over their estimate. (With pilot, the aircraft weighed approximately 750 pounds, thus

producing a wing loading of 1.47 pounds per square foot, about seventy-five percent greater than that of the 1902 glider. This increase in weight made the handling of the aircraft very different than for the earlier model.) The propellers would have to produce an extra ten pounds of thrust. Was it feasible?

And how was the machine to be launched? It was too heavy to be sent on its way by helpers at each wing tip. Wheels couldn't be added — both because of the weight and because the ground consisted of shifting, yielding sand. They decided on a small wheeled dolly, on a sixty-foot-long wooden track, that could be pointed into the wind. Chanute's colleague George Spratt was present and made himself useful by laying out the track.

By November 4, the new machine was ready for an engine test. A thrilling moment. After all their labors, powered flight was imminent.

Or was it? When Orville and Wilbur started up the engine, it kept missing, backfiring, jerking spasmodically as if it were about to quit. And it soon did. Both propellers broke loose, damaging their shafts. The brothers looked at each other, all too aware of the implications of this new problem. It would take weeks to repair the shafts.

Spratt started to pack, convinced that the two men from Dayton had missed their chance. Langley was even now preparing for a second attempt at powered flight, the first having failed because of trouble with the launching mechanism — not the aircraft itself, Langley declared. In a few days, the Aerodrome would be ready for a second launch. The long-suffering Manly would again be the pilot.

At Kill Devil Hills, the weather worsened and grew colder — "about zero, according to my backbone," Orville declared in a letter to Katharine. On November 5, Spratt returned to the mainland, taking with him the two damaged drive shafts. He promised to send them to Dayton by express at the first opportunity.

As Spratt left, Chanute arrived. The brothers' hospitality was strained, as their rations were severely depleted — "we had to come down to condensed milk and crackers for supper, with prospects of coffee and rice cakes for breakfast," Orville informed Katharine. The aircraft, bereft of power, sat forlornly in its shed.

Within a week or so — and perhaps because there was nothing to observe — Chanute cited pressing business demands and left, stopping long enough at Manteo to arrange for several pairs of gloves to be sent to the brothers, a welcome gift in the deepening chill on the Outer Banks. Despite the gesture, however, relations between the brothers and Chanute had deteriorated. Orville related in a letter to Katharine that the elderly Chanute "had been trying to purchase the Ader machine built by the French government at an expense of $100,000, which he was intending to have us fix up and *run* for him." The idea offended them, suggesting as it did a lack of faith in their prospects of flying. "He thinks we could do it! He doesn't seem to think our machines are so much superior as the manner in which we handle them. We are of just the reverse opinion. . . ."

On November 20, the new shafts arrived. But on the first test, the sprockets for the chain drive from the engine began to slip, in spite of heroic attempts at tightening. Finally, desperate, the brothers turned to "Arnstein's," a tire cement they had often used at the bicycle shop. It did the trick, securing the sprockets so effectively that they caused no more problems. Delighted, the brothers quickly installed them, then ran another engine test. But their delight quickly evaporated when the engine fired irregularly, subjecting the drive chains to violent tugs that threatened imminent breaks. It didn't take the Wrights long to unearth the reason: it lay in the method of feeding fuel to the engine. A few more adjustments. Now, at last, the engine was running well. Nothing stood in their way.

Samuel Pierpont Langley

Secretary of the prestigious Smithsonian Institution and a scientist of international reputation, Samuel Pierpont Langley developed an interest in flight in the 1890s. After successfully flying a scale-model "aerodrome" aircraft he had created, he secured $50,000 in funding from the U.S. War Department to create a full-sized Great Aerodrome. Out of ignorance — or perhaps out of arrogance — Langley ignored what Cayley, Lilienthal, and others had learned about airfoils. Despite several well-publicized attempts at flight, Langley's aeronautical contraption catapulted into the Potomac River in Washington — and with it sank Langley's career as a pioneer in flight.

Langley's Aerodrome

(Left) In 1896, Samuel Pierpont Langley astounded the world with his successful flight of a scale-model flying machine. Two years later, aided by a handsome military subsidy, he started work on a manned flying machine he called the Great Aerodrome.

"... a handful of mortar."

— Reporter at the scene, describing the flight of the Great Aerodrome

(Above) Langley, right, with Charles Manly, his test pilot, on launch day, October 7, 1903. (Top right) The Great Aerodrome, mounted on its catapult atop a houseboat. (Middle right) Takeoff. (Bottom right) Langley's wrecked Great Aerodrome floats in the Potomac.

Or so it seemed. Upon close examination of the propeller shafts, the brothers found a hairline crack. The shafts had let them down again. It was a sobering discovery. They realized that if they had attempted to take to the air, a shaft might have disintegrated, becoming a series of projectiles that would probably have ripped the aircraft apart, with goodness knows what consequences.

It says much for the Wrights' determination and courage that they didn't let this latest disappointment deter them. Aware that Langley was almost ready to test the Aerodrome for the second time, they knew their chances of being the first into the air were becoming slimmer by the day. Nevertheless,

they had to go on. Despite the steady onset of winter, they resolved to remain at Kitty Hawk long enough to attempt at least one flight. It was all coming down to a race against time.

On November 30, Orville left for Dayton, to make new shafts of spring steel. The weather deteriorated and a series of severe storms hit the Outer Banks. On December 9, Orville set off from Dayton on the return journey with the precious new shafts. While on the train, he read a newspaper account of the Aerodrome's latest attempted flight. Again, Charles Manly had settled himself in the repaired Aerodrome, run up the engine, and prepared for flight. Engine bellowing, the huge craft had trundled along the

track and into the air — whereupon it broke in two, the wreckage tumbling into the Potomac, a sorry mess of wire and wood. Again, Manly had managed to extricate himself from the deadly jumble of debris that threatened to take him to the bottom of the river. An assistant gallantly dived into the frigid water to help the pilot to safety. The Aerodrome was a complete write-off. Langley retired from the battle to be the first in manned flight.

Two hundred miles to the south, the Wrights installed the new propeller shafts. They had mixed feelings about Langley's catastrophe: on the one hand, they were relieved that the competition had been eliminated, at least for the moment; on the other, they felt an uncomfortable awareness that their attempt might be no more successful than Langley's had been.

The weather now was tranquil, for a change. In fact, too tranquil. The Flyer would never take to the air in such conditions. On December 13, the weather improved. A mild breeze rustled across the chilly sands. But the brothers didn't fly — they spent the day reading and walking. It was a Sunday and the Wrights had no intention of breaking the Sabbath for anything as trivial as an attempt to fly the world's first heavier-than-air machine. They had given their word to their father.

In late November 1903, while Samuel Pierpont Langley readied his cumbersome Great Aerodrome for flight hundreds of miles away, the Wrights' graceful Flyer sat expectantly outside the shed at Kitty Hawk.

On Monday, December 14, a small flag fluttered from the work shed: the prearranged signal to the lifesaving station that a powered flight was about to be attempted. Everyone was invited to watch. The Wrights wanted as many witnesses as could be mustered.

John Daniels, Robert Wescott, Thomas Beacham, W.S. Dough, and "Uncle Benny" O'Neal came out from the station and helped carry the hefty aircraft a quarter mile to the intended launch site. They made the job a little easier for themselves by using the sixty-foot track built for the takeoff run. Wilbur called it the "Junction Railroad." The job took forty minutes.

With the airplane's skids placed firmly on the launching dolly, they set about preparing her for flight. By now, the audience included two small boys and a dog, all three of whom scurried away when the engine clattered into life, emitting angry puffs of smoke.

Wilbur tossed a coin. He won. He clambered onto the lower wing, settling his hips snugly in the cradle that activated the wing-warping mechanism. He nodded. All set. Time to go. Orville stood at one wing tip, moving forward as the aircraft began to roll. The great wings shivered as if eager to get aloft. Then — lift! She rose from the track with an uncertain dignity, attaining an altitude of perhaps fifteen feet,

CHAPTER

7 TRIUMPH!

traveling some sixty feet beyond the track. She was flying! But not for long.

Slowing visibly, the airplane seemed to give up. With her engine still clattering away like a demented sewing machine, she lost height. The port wing hit the ground, swinging the aircraft around. The front skids dug into the sand. One broke. The flight had lasted just three and a half seconds.

Wilbur clambered out of the aircraft. The flight had succeeded, but it had been of pathetically brief duration. It couldn't even be considered a proper flight. No more than a hop, in fact. They would have to do better. Much better.

Thursday, December 17, dawned with a roar. A north wind battered the Wrights' camp. Puddles iced over. Casting worried glances at the turbulent sky, the brothers emerged, as natty as ever in suits, peaked caps, stiff white collars, and ties. They positioned the launching track into the wind. Five observers, including three from the lifesaving station, helped bring the aircraft to the track and position it for flight. The

(Below) Wilbur and Orville's ground crew and assorted children stand by as the Flyer sits on the track farther up Kill Devil Hills before the attempted flight on December 14, 1903.

brothers talked for a few minutes in a businesslike manner as if discussing the affairs of the bicycle shop; then they clasped hands. One spectator said it was as if they "weren't sure they'd ever see each other again." A poignant moment.

Orville, all business now, strode to the aircraft and settled himself on the lower wing, placing his feet on the footrest at the trailing edge, his hips in the cradle that provided control of the wing-warping mechanism and the rudder. He glanced at the instruments located close by: an anemometer to measure the distance traveled, a stopwatch, a Veedor engine-revolutions counter. The wind rocked the aircraft. The structure emitted tiny squeaks of complaint. All set.

(Below) At Kill Devil Hills, 10:35 A.M., December 17, 1903, Orville lifts off the sand in the first-ever manned flight. Wilbur, caught in half-stride, watches in amazement. The photograph, taken by John T. Daniels, one of the crew from the lifesaving station, became one of the most reproduced images of the twentieth century.

A flurry of waving hands from the lifesaving crew. A nod of encouragement from Wilbur.

Orville released the restraining wire. The little engine clattered and, vibrating, rattling, straining, the airplane began to trundle along the track, Wilbur trotting alongside to steady the right wing tip. About forty feet along the track, at a ground speed of approximately 6 MPH, the craft rose, dipped, climbed, then settled down for a smooth landing on the sand. It had lasted twelve seconds and had covered 120 feet.

It was over — the world's first powered, controlled flight. The brothers tried with only limited success to suppress their relief and delight. The countless hours, the nagging worries, the disappointments, the dangers; it was all justified, all infinitely worthwhile. Orville wrote that it was "the first time in the history of the world in which a machine carrying a man had raised itself by its own power into the air in full flight, had sailed forward without reduction of speed, and had finally landed at a point as high as that from which it had started."

The Wrights made three more flights that historic December day. (Top left) Orville flew about two hundred feet during their third flight. (Top right) Wilbur took the controls for the day's fourth and final flight. (Bottom) At the end of the fourth flight, Wilbur landed hard and broke the elevator support. He had flown for almost a minute and had covered a distance of 852 feet. (Inset) The triumphant telegram the brothers sent home.

THE WESTERN UNION TELEGRAPH COMPANY.
INCORPORATED
Form No. 168.   CABLE SERVICE TO ALL THE WORLD.
23,000 OFFICES IN AMERICA.
ROBERT C. CLOWRY, President and General Manager.

RECEIVED at

Via Norfolk Va

176 C KA CS 33 Paid.

Kitty Hawk N C Dec 17

Bishop M Wright

7 Hawthorne St

Success four flights thursday morning all against twenty one mile wind started from Level with engine power alone average speed through air thirty one miles longest 57 seconds inform Press home Christmas .

Orevelle Wright   525P

They flew three more times that day, each flight longer than the last, until Wilbur succeeded in covering 852 feet and remaining aloft for a remarkable fifty-nine seconds. But he landed hard and damaged the elevator. The lifesaving team helped carry the aircraft back to the campsite, where the brothers intended to repair the damage to the elevator and then make more flights.

They didn't get the chance. As they neared the camp, a violent gust of wind caught the machine and, with a kind of

other, rolling over and over, and me getting more tangled up in it all the time. I tell you, I was plumb scared. When the thing did stop for half a second, I nearly broke up every wire and upright getting out of it."

The incident, while annoying, did nothing to dim the brothers' delight. Or that of the faithful onlookers. One man dashed to the post office. "Damned if they ain't flew!" he announced breathlessly.

After sending their father a telegram telling him of their

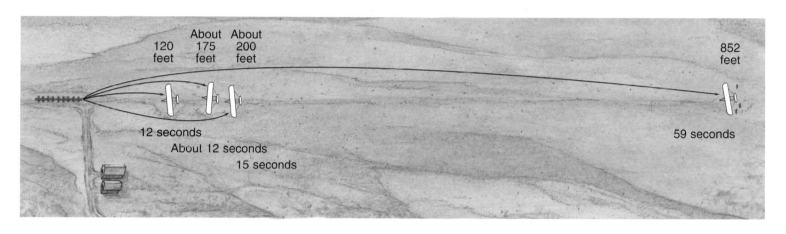

By increasing their distance during each of the three subsequent flights on December 17, 1903, Wilbur and Orville proved that their remarkable first flight was not a fluke.

deadly deliberation, flopped it upside down in the sand. Orville wrote: "The machine gradually turned over on us. Mr. Daniels, having no experience of handling a machine of this kind, hung on to it from the inside, and as a result was knocked down and turned over and over with it as it went. His escape was miraculous, as he was in with the engine and chains. The legs of the engine frame were all broken off, and the chain guides badly bent, a number of uprights and nearly all the rear ends of the ribs were broken. One spar only was broken." Daniels himself wrote: "I found myself caught in them wires and the machine blowing across the beach and heading for the ocean, landing first on one end and then the

triumph, the brothers began the task of dismantling the aircraft. They wanted to return to Dayton as soon as possible to enjoy Christmas with the family.

Although they had less than two minutes' powered flying time between them, Wilbur and Orville were the world's leading airmen as 1903 gave way to 1904. But they faced a dilemma. Wilbur wrote: "We found ourselves standing at a fork in the road. On the one hand, we could continue playing with the problem of flying so long as youth and leisure would permit but carefully avoiding those features which would require continuous effort and expenditure of considerable sums of money. On the other hand, we believed that if we would take the risk of devoting our entire time and financial resources, we could conquer the difficulties in our path to success before increasing years impaired our physical activity."

At the time, they were modestly well off, with close to $5,000 in two savings and loan associations in Dayton. The bicycle business had leveled off but the brothers didn't abandon it; rather, they eased themselves out of it, selling any bikes in production and handling any repair work that came in. Charlie Taylor could look after it, and did. The brothers themselves devoted all their energies to the new Flyer then under construction behind the shop. It would be bigger,

more powerful, and much stronger than the earlier aircraft.

The press continued to provoke the brothers. It was a case of no news or too much news, all of it absurdly inaccurate. Typical of the stories circulating in the days following the Kitty Hawk flights was this from the Norfolk *Virginian-Pilot*: "The machine flew for three miles. . . . Preparatory to its flight, the machine was placed on a platform . . . on a high sand hill and when all was in readiness, the fastenings of his machine were released. . . . The navigator, Wilbur Wright, then started a small gasoline engine which worked the propellers. When the edge of the incline was reached, the machine gradually rose

Why the Flyer Flew

The same plane and the same location. But one day, failure — and the next, success. Why?

The answer, strange as it seems, is that, like all of their contemporaries, Orville and Wilbur never actually did a proper job of designing a glider or a powered airplane.

Today, anyone designing an airplane needs to create a craft that can fly in a series of different conditions — at differing angles of incidence, air density, and wind speeds. Each variable affects other variables: wind speed affects lift; the size of the wing or the airfoil increases lift but adds to the weight; and so forth. It's a constant juggling of numbers. The Wrights left no notes, but probably from the time of their 1900 glider they set about their work differently.

At Kitty Hawk, they could safely assume wind speeds of 18 MPH — that was one of the reasons they went there. They probably also assumed an angle of incidence. That would have given them two constants. From this point, using Lilienthal's data, they could work out the airfoil they would need, the overall size of the wing needed to lift a plane carrying a pilot and a hefty aluminum engine (thanks to their corrected value for Smeaton's coefficient), and how much power that engine would have to produce to get the plane up to flying speed.

But, most of all, they needed that wind.

WRIGHT BROS. FIRST POWER DRIVEN PLANE
FIRST FLIGHT AT KITTY HAWK IN 1903

ORVILLE WRIGHT

WILBUR WRIGHT

On December 14, with winds of just 7 to 8 MPH, the momentum of the plane carried it off the rail, but it was not yet at flying speed, so it stalled. A rough estimate suggests that the takeoff distance in still air was at least 150 to 200 feet and possibly more. (Small wonder many early aviators spoke of the "takeoff problem" facing heavier-than-air craft — imagine these machines racing over the earth until somehow they gained flying speed!)

On December 17, the wind speed was about 25 to 27 MPH. It was gusty, almost a gale, but the Wrights had glided in winds of up to 37 MPH. The Flyer hit 6 to 8 MPH by the end of the track, the head winds did the rest — and the first powered flight took off.

until it obtained [sic] an altitude of 60 feet. . . . Protruding from the center of the car is a huge fan-shaped rudder of canvas, stretched upon a frame of wood. . . ."

Orville described the story as "ninety-nine percent wrong." Other accounts were no better. Many papers chose to ignore the Wrights' accomplishment altogether, convinced that it was just another "stunt." The Cincinnati *Enquirer* ran banner headlines about the Wrights; whereas the Dayton *Journal* made no mention of the story. Octave Chanute in Chicago knew nothing about the Wrights' success until Katharine informed him.

Orville wrote: "Since our return, we have been receiving daily offers of stocking our company for us from some of these professional promoters who would like to get a chance to swindle some of the people who think there is an immense fortune in the flying machine. Even our friend Herring has made us a very generous offer, a copy of which I am making for your amusement. . . ."

Ever the opportunist, Herring was claiming to be the world's first airman — but, acknowledging the Wrights' contribution, he offered them equal shares in the company he said he intended to form.

Early in January, the Wrights, still bedeviled by inaccurate press reports, issued the following statement to the Associated Press: "It has not been our intention to make any detailed public statement concerning the private trials of our power Flyer on the 17th of December last; but since the contents of a private telegram, announcing to our folks at home the success of our trials, was dishonestly communicated to the newspaper-

men at the Norfolk office, and led to the imposition to the public, by persons who never saw the Flyer or its flights, of a fictitious story incorrect in almost every detail; and since this story together with several pretended interviews or statements, which were fakes pure and simple, have been very widely disseminated, we feel impelled to make some correction. The real facts were as follows: 'On the morning of December 17th, between the hours of 10:30 o'clock and noon, four flights were made, two by Orville Wright and two by Wilbur Wright. The starts were all made from a point on the level sand about two hundred feet west of our camp, which is located a quarter of a mile north of the Kill Devil sand hill, in Dare County, North Carolina. . . .'"

AP sent out the story but omitted the opening paragraph, which infuriated the Wrights. A few days later, Wilbur's blood pressure soared again when he wrote to the editor of the *Independent*, complaining of "the most unmitigated impudence" in the paper's February 4 issue in which an article — a "cut and paste" concoction of extracts from Wilbur's speeches to the Western Society of Engineers — had been published under his name. Wilbur made it clear that "I have never given to any person permission or encouragement to palm off as an original article extracts from these copyrighted addresses and newspaper dispatches. Neither have I given to the *Independent*, nor to any one, the least permission or excuse for using my name in the furtherance of such attempted fraud. . . ."

If the people at the *Independent* felt badly about the incident, they never said so.

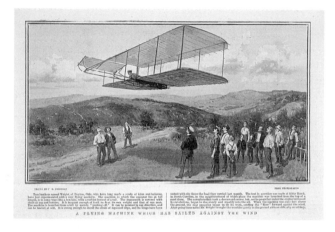

Popular depictions of the Wright brothers' first flights mixed fancy and falsehood.

A New Base of OPERATIONS

"We are in a large meadow.... In addition to cattle there have been a dozen or more horses in the pasture ... and we have been at much trouble to get them safely away before making trials."

— Wilbur Wright to Octave Chanute,
June 21, 1904

The passengers on the Dayton, Springfield & Urbana Railway usually gazed stolidly out the windows or read their papers as they traveled the rural route. There was little to see but an endless procession of trees and farms and tiny towns. In the spring of 1904, however, as the interurban slowed to a stop at the Simms Station near Dayton, something unusual caught their attention. Something poking its odd-looking nose out of the shed that had been built in the winter months.

Orville, left, and Wilbur in the spring of 1904 with the improved Flyer at their new base of operations, a pasture just outside Dayton known locally as Huffmann Prairie.

A few of the passengers got to their feet to see more clearly. One man said it was those crazy Wrights working on their flying machine — the most notable feature of which was that it didn't fly. It had been squatting there for weeks, looking like a cross between a tent and a windjammer. Everyone had a chuckle about this because, as was well known, people who experimented with flying machines were just about the craziest galoots in captivity.

But one man declared that he believed the reports . . . sort of. The Wrights had flown. He was sure of it. But his face reddened as he said it. More chuckles. More wiseacres declaring that it must have been an optical illusion, all done with mirrors, a regular Houdini stunt. A second man said he had read about the brothers from Dayton in a Cincinnati paper. Another declared that a friend of his had a friend who had actually seen the Wrights fly. No, not here, but in North Carolina. A burly fellow, a farmer by the look of him, was of the opinion that the experimenters wouldn't succeed because they hadn't attached a balloon to their craft. Much nodding from the assembled travelers. Everyone knew that the way to make a flying machine fly was to attach a balloon.

In a few minutes, the trolley had departed for Dayton.

As soon as the trolley was out of sight, two men emerged from the shed. In business suits and caps, they didn't look like aviators, more like bankers. Nevertheless, they trundled their airplane into the open and started the motor. It clattered into life, its chains rattling, then puffed and popped into silence. Nothing the two men could do would revive it.

The two men continued to labor on the engine, but it remained lifeless. They consulted their pocket watches and the trolley timetable. Time to switch off the motor and get the airplane back in the shed. Another train was coming with another load of curious passengers.

During the winter of 1903–04, the Wrights went to work on the design of a new airplane, one that would have more power and a much less sensitive elevator. Now that the world (or at least some of it) knew what the Wrights had accomplished at Kitty Hawk, there was little need for secrecy — and, in fact, little need for Kitty Hawk. They looked for a proving ground nearer to home. It didn't take long. Torrence Huffmann, president of the Fourth National Bank of Dayton, offered them the use of his farmland a few miles outside the city, a pasture known as Huffmann Prairie, not far from Simms Station, a stop on the interurban trolley that ran between Dayton and Springfield, Ohio. Although far from perfect, dotted as it was with trees and power lines, the hundred-acre plot possessed one important advantage: it was free.

Wilbur wrote to Chanute: "At Kitty Hawk, we had unlimited space and wind enough to make starting easy with a short track. If the wind was very light, we could utilize the hills if necessary in getting the initial velocity. Here, we must depend on a long track, and light winds or even dead calms. We are in a large meadow . . . skirted on the west and north by trees. This not only shuts off the wind somewhat but also gives a slight downtrend. . . . Also, the ground is an old swamp and is filled with grassy hummocks some six inches high so that it resembles a prairie-dog town. . . ."

The engine on the first Flyer tended to overheat, losing power. Now the brothers decided to build two engines, each with four cylinders. Both had more space around the cylinders, enhancing the efficiency of the cooling system. They also sketched out an eight-cylinder model but chose not to proceed with it.

The latter days of May 1904 saw the completion of the new engine and airplane. It was outwardly similar to the previous year's machine but was heavier and had a slightly modified airfoil section. The Wrights saw the first flight of the new

model as something of an occasion. The bishop, then aged seventy-five, made the trip out to Huffmann's pasture with his eldest son Lorin and his family. A handful of reporters from the Dayton and Cincinnati newspapers also showed up, invited by the brothers with the proviso that they not write sensational stories or take any photographs.

The audience expected great things. But the frustrated Wright brothers found themselves unable to deliver. Everything went wrong. It rained all morning. The wind, never as reliable as on the Outer Banks of North Carolina, kept dying, preventing takeoff. Then the rain moved in again. On top of everything else, the engine failed repeatedly. Two attempted takeoffs ended in ignominious failure. One saw the Flyer galloping the length of the track, only to come to a weary halt before reaching the end.

The brothers did manage one flight in which they climbed to an altitude of six feet — then landed immediately due to loss of power. Scathing newspaper reports might have been expected, but they didn't materialize. (It has been suggested that the Wrights failed deliberately in order to deter

press attention. Certainly, a letter written by Wilbur some years later tends to support this theory. Writing about forthcoming demonstrations, he commented: "No doubt an attempt will be made to spy upon us while we are making the trial flight . . . but we have already thought out a plan which we are certain will baffle such efforts as neatly as we fooled the newspapers during the two seasons we were experimenting at Simms." Details of the "plan" were never divulged.)

The 1904 Flyer continued to be a disappointment. Its reluctance to climb resulted in dangerous situations. On one

would thrust their aircraft forward with sufficient velocity to ensure a takeoff every time. It consisted of a tower that resembled a small derrick, with a system of pulleys hauling a weight of eight hundred pounds (later increased to fourteen hundred). A group of helpers would heave on the rope, lifting the weight to the top of the tower. On a signal, they would release the cord; the weight would plummet, pulling the line that went under the track, propelling the airplane forward. Now the Wrights were no longer dependent upon brisk winds to get their Flyer into the air.

(Left) For reasons Orville and Wilbur didn't understand at first, the 1904 Flyer performed poorly and never gained much altitude. (Opposite) The plane shed then, and rebuilt today. (Pages 84–85) It took nineteen attempts before the Flyer finally took to the skies. Unreliable winds and repeated engine failure added to the brothers' problems.

occasion, Orville stalled the Flyer but the tail-heavy airplane descended gently and wasn't damaged. Interestingly, Orville reported an odd tapping noise, "as if some part of the machine were loose and flapping." They examined the Flyer carefully, but could find nothing that could have caused the noise. As any modern-day pilot will agree, the Wrights had encountered "buffeting," the classic symptom of an impending stall.

The generally feeble winds encountered in the Dayton area that summer severely limited the brothers' flights, as did the length of the takeoff run permitted by the "Junction Railroad." So the Wrights created a launching device that

A highlight of the year 1904 was the St. Louis Fair, which commemorated the hundredth anniversary of the Louisiana Purchase. A staggering prize of $100,000 was offered for the first aircraft — airplane or airship — to fly around the fairground, a distance of ten miles. Most people expected the expatriate Brazilian, Alberto Santos-Dumont, to win with his new airship that had enjoyed some success in Paris. In February, the Wrights journeyed to St. Louis to look the site over — and promptly abandoned their plans to participate. They didn't like the layout, which seemed to have been built with airships, rather than airplanes, in mind.

Back in Ohio, Wilbur and Orville became a familiar sight on the trolley as they journeyed back and forth from Dayton to Huffmann Prairie. They chatted openly with the locals about their flights and their problems. One individual, Amos I. Root, the editor and publisher of a beekeeping magazine, was fascinated by the Wrights and their flying machine. In September, he drove his automobile from Medina, Ohio, near Akron, to Dayton (a formidable journey in those days). He arranged for accommodation with a family living close to Huffmann Prairie. On September 20, Mr. Root witnessed a remarkable feat — the first complete circle flown by an airplane. He called it "one of the grandest sights, if not the grandest sight, of my life." He went on effusively: "Imagine a locomotive that had left its track, and is climbing up in the air right toward you — a locomotive without any wheels we will say, but with white wings instead. . . . Well now, imagine this white locomotive, with wings that spread twenty feet each way, coming right toward you with a tremendous flap of its propellers, and you will have something like what I saw."

With more than a little prescience, Mr. Root declared that the Wrights "have probably not even a faint glimpse of what their discovery is going to bring to the children of men. No one living can give a guess of what is coming along this line, much better than any one living could conjecture the final outcome of Columbus's experiment when he pushed off through the trackless waters." He closed with a stern warning, with which no one could argue: "No drinking man should ever be allowed to undertake to run a flying machine."

Root sent a copy of his article to the *Scientific American* and gave the editor permission to use it in any way he saw fit. It never appeared.

On December 1, 1904, Orville flew for an impressive five minutes and eight seconds, traveling about three miles. The brothers did not realize that their earlier disappointments had been due largely to high temperature combined with high humidity, plus an engine that delivered too little power. The air

". . . Imagine this white locomotive, with wings that spread twenty feet each way, coming right toward you with a tremendous flap of its propellers, and you will have something like what I saw."

— Amos I. Root, 1904

simply couldn't support the aircraft — and in the prevailing conditions, the engine produced even less power than in cooler weather. It was another of the riddles concerning air that began to unravel as the brothers acquired more knowledge of the element they were attempting to conquer.

By the end of 1904, the Wrights felt they had accomplished what they'd set out to do. Now, it was time to garner some rewards. During their visit to St. Louis earlier in the year, Colonel John B. Capper of the British army had asked them to submit a proposal to the British government.

Early in January 1905, Wilbur called on his congressman, Robert M. Nevin, seeking his counsel on how to approach the U.S. War Department. Patriotic citizens, the Wrights wanted their government to have an opportunity to acquire the airplane before it went abroad: "It not only flies through the air at high speed," Wilbur wrote, "but also lands without being wrecked. During the year 1904, one hundred and five flights were made at our experimenting station on the Huffmann

Prairie, east of the city; and though our experience in handling the machine has been too short to give any high degree of skill, we nevertheless succeeded, toward the end of the season, in making two flights of five minutes each, in which we sailed round and round the field until a distance of about three miles had been covered, at a speed of thirty-five miles an hour. . . . The numerous flights in straight lines, in circles, and over S-shaped courses, in calms and in winds have made it quite certain that flying has been brought to a point where it can be made of great practical use in various ways, one of which is that of scouting and carrying messages in time of war. If the latter features are of interest to our own government, we shall be pleased to take up the matter either on a basis of providing machines of agreed specification, at a contract price, or of furnishing all the scientific and practical information we have accumulated in these years of experimenting, together with a license to use our patents; thus putting the government in a position to operate on its own account. . . ."

By November 1904, Orville and Wilbur had made considerable progress with their aircraft. They could now keep the Flyer up for minutes at a time and maneuver it into graceful circles over the field.

Congressman Nevin promptly contacted the newly appointed Secretary of War, William Howard Taft. The response the Wrights received appeared to be a form letter, saying that many requests had been received for financial assistance in the development of flying machines and that the Board was not interested in designs until they had been "brought to the stage of practical operation." This was precisely what the Wrights had done, but no one at the War Department seemed to comprehend the fact. Meanwhile, an invitation to submit terms was received from London. The Wrights replied immediately, stating their willingness to sign a contract for an aircraft capable of carrying two people fifty miles at a speed of no less than thirty miles an hour. The Wrights' offer also included pilot training and construction details. The price was a hefty $2,500 per mile for every mile flown in the trial. But it would have been a bargain — a mere $125,000 for a head start over the rest of the world. Incredibly, the British military experts shook their heads, unable to appreciate the benefits of the new invention.

The French came next, to negotiate a contract calling for the delivery of an airplane at a cost of one million francs (then, about $200,000) for the French army. A few months later, a French army officer and aviation enthusiast, Captain Ferdinand Ferber, made contact with the Wrights. But they weren't sure whether he represented the French government, a group of businessmen, or even wealthy sportsmen from the Aéro-Club. It all looked very hopeful, but the deal fell through the following spring.

So far, the Wrights had not made a penny from their airplane.

The first weeks of 1905 saw little but storms, heavy rains, ice, and snow in the Dayton area. And when the brothers were able to take to the air again, in June, they still had trouble executing turns. "We have made several changes in the operating handles," Wilbur informed Chanute in July, "and

have had some trouble instantly acquiring familiarity with them. We are sure they will be a good thing when we have learned the combination properly, but they have cost us several rather unlucky breakages, aggregating several weeks of delay."

Sometimes, the aircraft would turn — then refuse to come out of the maneuver. One or two minor crashes were attributed to this phenomenon. Was there something basically wrong with their design, or could it be their lack of skill in piloting? They decided to try disconnecting the rudder and wing-warping controls and adding a separate lever to control the rudder. They reasoned that if the vertical rudder were controlled independently, the Flyer's stability about its vertical axis would have to be increased. At last, they had come close to solving the problem of turns.

Wilbur wrote: "The trouble was really due to the fact that in circling, the machine has to carry the load resulting from centrifugal force, in addition to its own weight. . . . The machine in question had but a slight surplus of power above what was required for straight flight, and as the additional load caused by circling increased rapidly as the circling became smaller, a limit was finally reached beyond which the machine was no longer able to maintain sufficient speed to sustain itself in the air. . . . When we had discovered the real nature of the trouble, and knew that it could always be remedied by tilting the machine forward a little, so that its flying speed would be restored [avoiding stall], we felt we were ready to place flying machines on the market."

The brothers had abandoned the bicycle business by this time; Charlie Taylor spent most of his days in the workshop making or repairing parts for the Flyer. When the weather improved, they flew — and found the new controls dangerously complicated. Orville crashed on July 14, 1905, and broke the upper wing. Luckily, he escaped injury. In August, the elevator was increased in size from fifty to eighty-four square feet and positioned a full twelve feet ahead of the wings. Hoping to make steering easier, the Wrights increased the size of the vertical rudder from twenty to thirty-five square feet.

Early in September, Wilbur took off and flew four full circuits of the field; a day later, he flew the first figure eight. The weather deteriorated and the brothers retired to the hangar to modify the Flyer, eliminating the droop (anhedral) of the wings and making a new set of propellers. The Wrights had been dissatisfied with the performance of the original propellers, suspecting that they were twisting in flight. In their tireless, meticulous way, they set out to prove their contention by mounting small elevator-like surfaces behind each propeller — "little jokers," they called them. It was a fairly simple matter to set them at an angle so as to reduce the pitch of the propeller and balance the pressure that seemed to be distorting the blades. This research led to the manufacture of propellers with a backward sweep, which solved the problem.

The new Flyer was completed by the end of September. It was the world's first practical airplane — one with separate pitch, roll, and yaw controls. The Wrights flew it repeatedly in the early fall, circling the field at Huffmann Prairie again and again. Hundreds of locals witnessed the flights. For the passengers on the interurban, the aircraft became a common sight. Soon, inevitably, the press became interested. By early October, the papers were full of stories about the sensational goings-on near Dayton — incredible flights of more than half an hour, during which the aircraft traveled in excess of twenty miles.

Now, at this moment of triumph, the Wrights abruptly ceased all flying.

Frustrated by the American government's lack of interest — or, more properly, comprehension — and convinced that everyone was trying to cheat them, Orville and Wilbur decided that the only way to protect what they had created was to keep it secret until a proper business deal could be arranged.

Meanwhile, they continued to work on the Flyer, adding more power and upright seating, but adamantly refused to disclose any plans or photographs. In the spring of 1907, Wilbur sailed for Europe to explore business possibilities in

On September 29, 1905, the Wrights proved to a large crowd of spectators that they had, indeed, mastered the dynamics of flight. Their new Flyer flew steadily for over half an hour and executed intricate figure eights and turns. The world now had its first fully operational aircraft.

London, Paris, and Berlin. Orville and Charlie Taylor followed later. The brothers had a Flyer shipped to France in a crate, secure from prying eyes. Had the Wrights flown the machine in Europe, they would have had the continent at their feet.

At about this time, the brothers tried again to interest the United States Army, stating that they were prepared to furnish a machine capable of flying one hundred miles with one person on board. The army's Board of Ordnance and

The First Practical Flying Machine

The 1905 Flyer was a graceful machine. From the simple fitting attaching a strut on the upper wing (left) to the precise stitching on the fabric covering (right, top), the Wrights' careful preparation and technical acumen are evident everywhere. (Right, middle) A propeller hub on the new Flyer bears its year of completion. (Right, bottom) In addition to major changes, the 1905 Flyer also boasted many minor improvements. Previously, the wing-warping lines ran through pulleys; the 1905 model featured small sections of bicycle chain, mounted on sprockets. (Opposite) The mounts for the 1905 airplane's enlarged canard.

However excited and satisfied the Wrights were with the first flights in December 1903, they knew their accomplishment was only the first step toward practical powered flying. Yes, they had flown — but their flight was straight and level, and they had stayed close to the ground. There were no turns, no climbing and descent, and only minimal use of the controls.

For the next twenty-one months, Wilbur and Orville refined the design of the Flyer and, in October 1905, they felt they had finally developed a practical flying machine.

The 1905 Flyer boasted a number of significant modifications. Gone was the anhedral (downward slope) in the wings that had helped make the 1903 Flyer so unstable in terms of roll. To fix a later problem with undulations

created when the plane's nose bobbed up and down, the Wrights had moved the canard forward and enlarged it — giving the plane marginally reduced stability in pitch but superior control. Perhaps most important, the controls for the rudder and wing warping were now operated independently. This made the pilot's job busier, but gave him better control in turns. As well, once the two controls were independent of each other, Wilbur concluded that the aft tail, meant to control yaw, had been too small, so its area was increased and then it was moved rearward by about two feet, which improved the plane's directional stability.

The 1905 Flyer was restored by Orville in the 1940s, and is on display today at Carillon Park in Dayton, Ohio.

Fortification sent the Wrights essentially the same letter they had sent Congressman Nevin a few months earlier. At the same time, inquiries to their contacts in Britain and France produced no concrete proposals.

The Wrights had first applied for a patent on their invention in 1903, only to be rebuffed by the Patent Office because they had bypassed the legal profession. They contacted a patent attorney named Harry A. Toulmin. Shortly afterward, the Wrights received a letter from an individual who claimed to have patented an airplane; he suggested that they form a company to market the Flyer — "a two-thirds interest for you two and a one-third interest for me." The writer was none other than Augustus Herring, Chanute's former associate. The Wrights ignored the letter, but they hadn't heard the last of the opportunistic Mr. Herring.

The brothers' absence from the flying scene for close to three years resulted — inevitably — in others stepping into the limelight. Glenn Curtiss of Hammondsport, New York, was a few years younger than the Wrights, and, by coincidence, had also been involved in the cycle business. He owned three bicycle shops and became a champion cyclist before graduating to the construction of motorcycle engines in the late 1890s. In 1907, one of his machines broke all records by reaching 136.29 MPH. The following year, Alexander Graham Bell contacted him and purchased two Curtiss engines for use by the Aerial Experiment Association, a group of enthusiastic aeronautical experimenters under Bell's chairmanship. The Secretary of the AEA was U.S. Army Lieutenant Thomas E. Selfridge. The Association soon had several aircraft in the air: the Red Wing, piloted by Canadian F.W. "Casey" Baldwin; the June Bug, piloted by Curtiss himself, in which he won the $2,500 silver trophy offered by the journal *Scientific American*; and the Silver Dart, designed and flown by another Canadian, John McCurdy, in partnership with Curtiss.

The AEA aircraft had a form of roll control, using movable tip ailerons. Bell himself lost no time in steering clear of any controversy with the Wright brothers: "I do not know exactly the circumstances that led to the adoption of the movable wing tips, as I was in Washington at the time; but if, as I have reason to believe, their adoption was due to a suggestion of mine that movable wing tips should be used, contained in a letter to Mr. Baldwin, I may say that this suggestion was made without any knowledge upon my part of anything the Wright brothers may have done."

Curtiss said, "We were familiar with the warping wing system of the Wrights and we hoped to develop some other system of balance. . . . The second machine was fitted with what we afterwards called ailerons. . . ." Lieutenant Selfridge had earlier written to the Wrights, asking for information about their aircraft. Wilbur had replied, referring to the 1906 patent in which wing warping was described in detail. No doubt believing that they had circumvented the Wrights' patent, Curtiss installed mid-wing ailerons on the AEA aircraft. The Wrights objected and informed Curtiss that he had violated their patent; they would bring suit if he persisted in exhibiting or indulging in any commercial exploitation of the Wrights' invention. They offered him the opportunity to operate under license. Curtiss's reply was curt: he had no intention of "entering the exhibition business," he declared, referring the matter of patents to Selfridge, the secretary of the AEA. It was the beginning of a series of bitter legal squabbles between the Wrights and Curtiss that would fester for more than a decade.

The AEA's last aircraft, the Silver Dart, first took to the air late in 1908, powered by an engine of 50 HP, weighing a little over two hundred pounds. It was equal to the best of the French engines of that time. The Silver Dart represented a striking leap forward.

A few months earlier, there had been encouraging

(Above) Canadian John McCurdy soars over Bras d'Or Lake in the Silver Dart he designed in partnership with Glenn Curtiss. (Below, left) Glenn Curtiss, seated at the controls of one of his own planes. In 1908, he piloted the June Bug (below, right) in a one-hour sustained flight.

developments for the brothers from Dayton. The U.S. Army Signal Corps decided that perhaps they should have the Wright airplane after all. Within a few weeks, the Wrights had a contract with Lazare Weiller, a well-to-do Frenchman, to form a syndicate controlling the rights to build, sell, or license the use of the Wright aircraft in France. The new company would be known as La Compagnie Générale de Navigation Aérienne. But Orville and Wilbur had held out too long, and they received significantly less than they had originally demanded. Back in America, the Signal Corps specified the need for an airplane capable of carrying two men and fuel for a flight of 125 miles at a speed of at least 40 MPH. It was a proposal the Wrights could meet, not surprisingly, given that, through connections, Wilbur himself had had a hand in drafting the request. The Wrights set to work on the new

machine, but first decided to return to Kitty Hawk to hone their flying skills, which hadn't been tested for several years.

The brothers arrived at their old campsite early in May 1908 and were shocked by the sight that greeted them. The sagging remnants of buildings were hardly recognizable as the place they had lived in for so many months; the elements had wrecked everything. The camp would have to be erected anew. And there were newspaper reporters to contend with as well. The Norfolk *Virginian-Pilot* declared that one of the brothers had flown ten miles out over the ocean. Other news services picked up the story and it soon appeared all over the world.

The first reporter to reach Kitty Hawk was D. Bruce Salley, a freelance writer from Norfolk, Virginia. Before heading there, Salley had contacted the New York *Herald*, hoping for a commission to write an article about the Wrights. But the

(Opposite) By 1908, the old campsite at Kitty Hawk had become dilapidated. (Above) The latest version of the Flyer sits on the sand dunes, ready for testing and practice. Five years after the historic first flight, the Wrights now had a plane that could climb to one hundred feet and stay aloft for over an hour at a time.

Herald simply took Salley's suggestion and sent their leading reporter, Byron R. Newton, to cover the story. Soon, several other correspondents showed up at the campsite, representing the New York *American*, the London *Daily Mail*, and *Collier's Weekly*.

Most of the visitors were pests, but not all. Charles W. Furnas, a capable mechanic from Dayton, walked into the camp and offered his services in any capacity. The Wrights lost no time in putting him to work and were delighted with his contributions. On May 14, Wilbur took Furnas for a flight; thus, the mechanic from Dayton became the world's first airplane passenger.

Shortly afterward, Wilbur had a serious crash after stalling the Flyer. Although he practically demolished the aircraft, he was lucky to survive with nothing worse than bruises and cuts. The resolute brothers seemed to accept these disasters and the injuries resulting from them like patients undergoing necessary but painful medical treatment. It was the price of progress.

Wilbur's crash ended the flying season at Kitty Hawk. And the brothers had work to do back in Dayton. The Signal Corps trials were to be held at Fort Myer, Virginia, in September. The French then informed the Wrights that no more delays would be tolerated; they must come to France to demonstrate their airplane. Wilbur and Orville discussed the matter. They decided that Wilbur would journey to France; Orville would return to Dayton to prepare for the Signal Corps tests.

When Wilbur arrived in France on May 28, 1908, he became the catalyst of a revolution.

Hubris & High FLYERS

*"All the French have aviation in their blood. . . . Foreigners may
one day equal our machines, but never our aviators."*

— Alfred Leblanc, 1905

It was a curious fact that, although the airplane had been invented in the United States, much of the world regarded Paris as the aviation capital of the world. Possibly the reason was the city's long association with lighter-than-air flight. Hadn't the Montgolfier brothers conducted many of their ballooning experiments in the city after their first flights in the south of France in 1783? Clearly, it was France's destiny to be the world's leader in aeronautics: "All the French have aviation in their blood. . . . Foreigners may one day equal our machines, but never our aviators. In order to know how to fly, it's necessary to possess the qualities that constitute our national patrimony," asserted Alfred Leblanc. Then how had those Yankees, Wilbur and Orville Wright, accomplished so much without a drop of French blood between them?

To the majority of French citizens, the distinction between balloons, airships, and airplanes was vague indeed. But not to Captain Ferdinand Ferber, a career officer in the French army. Ferber taught basic courses in ballistics at L'Ecole d'Application de Fontainbleau and seemed in every way typical of his ilk. But he had a grand passion — flying. An admirer of Lilienthal, he had built his first aircraft, a kite,

in the summer of 1898. The indefatigable captain then built three more, one of which managed reasonably good glides when he jumped from a platform. Ferber's gliders were monoplanes shaped like polygonal kites without tails. Although he began his flying tests at the same time as the Wrights, he soon lagged far behind them in technical accomplishments. His aircraft were crude and lacked effective controls at a time when the Wrights had mastered control of their gliders — in pitch, with their canard surface, and in roll, by wing warping. Ferber heard Octave Chanute's 1903 lecture to the Aéro-Club de France and did his best to obtain an invitation to the Wrights' camp at Kill Devil Hills. In this, he was unsuccessful.

In March 1904, near Calais, Ferber experimented with his latest glider, based on the Wright design. Results were disappointing, largely because he neglected to incorporate the Wrights' system of control. At about the same time, a well-to-do member of the Aéro-Club in Paris, Irish-born Ernest Archdeacon, was offering attractive prizes for outstanding flights: the Archdeacon Cup for the first powered flight of twenty-five meters in France; 1,500 francs for the

(Left) Captain Ferdinand Ferber brings one of his elaborate gliders in for a landing at Nice, France, on January 15, 1902.

A Frenchman's Passion for Flying

Captain Ferdinand Ferber (left) built numerous gliders and powered craft, including some (above) loosely based on the Wrights' designs. But he is remembered more for the enthusiasm for aviation he helped foster in France — with support from organizations like the Aéro-Club de France (his membership card, left) and wealthy patrons who established lucrative incentive prizes to reward French flying achievements.

first powered flight of one hundred meters; and the Deutsch-Archdeacon prize of 50,000 francs for the first flight in a closed circuit of one kilometer in Europe. The thinking seemed to be that if sufficient funds were tossed at the country's aviators, they would inevitably accomplish world-beating flights.

Meanwhile, in April 1904, Ferber found himself posted to the balloon station at Le Parc de Chalais in Meudon, a Paris suburb. The commandant, Colonel Charles Renard, a balloon and airship enthusiast, promised to support Ferber in his experiments with heavier-than-air flight. Over the next few months, Ferber devised an ingenious launching system for his aircraft, consisting of three tall pylons. By means of pulleys and ropes, he could lift a glider some thirty feet in the air and release it for testing. Unfortunately, the authorities regarded Ferber's work as a military secret and little information became available to the public.

While at Nice, Ferber had built aircraft No. 6. Soon after arriving at Meudon, he made a number of modifications, adding an aft horizontal stabilizer and a pair of wheels to facilitate landings. No. 6 now boasted forward and aft horizontal tails, although only the forward canard was controllable. Ferber's aircraft lacked any form of roll control, but he was experimenting with jibs placed at the wing tips. Without a vertical tail, his aircraft had a tendency to skid and probably exhibited yaw oscillations. Ferber's basic design, with a vertical tail, subsequently saw service with Alberto Santos-Dumont and Voisin in France, as well as with Glenn Curtiss in the United States.

Ferber had installed an engine in No. 6. Producing 6 HP, it drove two coaxial tractor propellers but was hopelessly underpowered. He obtained another engine, this one producing 12 HP, and installed it in airplane No. 6 — which was then redesignated No. 7. On May 27, 1905, Ferber launched the new aircraft from his pylons and executed a powered glide, the glide ratio being reduced from 1:5 to 1:7. It was the first powered flight in Europe, but because of the military's insistence on secrecy, only a handful of people knew about it.

The 1903 Flyer had been a dangerously unstable aircraft that no one but the Wrights could have flown. They succeeded because they had invested a lot of time in learning to fly the machines they built. During 1904 and most of 1905, they pursued an intensive, carefully planned program of development and flying — modifying and improving their aircraft to enhance their performance and usefulness. On October 5, 1905, Wilbur flew for thirty-eight minutes, three seconds under complete control, traveling approximately fifteen miles. The flight ended only when the fuel supply was exhausted. It was a highly significant flight, although few realized it at the time. The Wrights had succeeded in producing the world's first practical aircraft, capable of carrying two people for over an hour.

In France, Ferber was in something of a slump. His patron, Renard, had died unexpectedly and Ferber now received little support from his superiors. His experiments were curtailed, although he still flew his machine on powered glides. During this time, he was using a single propeller, but this induced a rotation of the aircraft during powered glides. To compensate, Ferber added movable jibs at the wing tips. Unfortunately, he oriented the surfaces incorrectly and they were of little use.

This was yet another example of the extraordinary inability of the French to solve the problem of control. A highly innovative French pioneer, Robert Esnault-Pelterie, wrote in the journal *L'Aérophile*, describing his experience with his replica of the Wright 1902 glider. He'd tried to duplicate the performance claimed by the brothers from Dayton and when he was unable to do so, he blamed it on the wing-warping feature and proposed movable horizontal surfaces instead.

Thus, the Frenchman invented ailerons, not realizing that an Englishman, M.P.W. Boulton, had already done so back in 1859. Another Englishman, Richard Harte, had proposed hinged flaps on the trailing edge of a wing, an advanced idea in 1870. But these two innovations were never used; in fact, it seems certain that none of the early aviation pioneers knew anything of these developments. (Esnault-Pelterie was a remarkable character; even at this early stage of aeronautical development, he was considering the possibilities of space travel and jet engines.)

In 1905, the French talked and wrote a lot about the supposed inadequacies of the Wright machine. They still nurtured hopes of wresting the lead from the Wrights and restoring France's preeminent position in the aeronautical world. Ferber alone continued to work to produce a fully controllable airplane, but it wasn't easy, given the attitude of his superiors. And he failed to appreciate the value of Esnault-Pelterie's work — which was eventually developed by Santos-Dumont and Blériot in France, as well as by Curtiss in the United States, to produce the first modern ailerons. Early in October, the Wrights wrote to Ferber, at last expressing interest in licensing rights to their airplane. Ferber responded immediately with an offer to buy — with the proviso that, in view of his own successes, the price should be reduced. The Wrights' reply was a masterpiece of tact. The brothers congratulated Ferber on his work: "Probably no one in the world can appreciate as much as we can the importance of your results. . . . France is fortunate to have a Ferber."

Thanks to the captain's work, France would be in a better position to make practical use of the Wright airplane. Accordingly, they quoted a reduced price of one million francs (then about $200,000) to the French government, to be paid following a demonstration flight of at least fifty kilometers in one hour or less. It was a bargain, and considerably less than the Wrights' offer to the British government.

During this correspondence, the Wrights made an unfortunate (though accurate) comment about the political situation in Europe, observing that Germany's Kaiser Wilhelm was in a "truculent mood." The brothers would come to regret the remark.

Meanwhile, Ferber was telling his superiors about the remarkable accomplishments of the Wright airplane. The generals were skeptical, doubting that a junior officer, a mere captain of artillery, could be aware of all these developments when they had heard nothing. Why had the subject never been broached in the press?

Frustrated, Ferber showed the Wrights' letter to Ernest Archdeacon, the Irish-born lawyer who lived in Paris. It was a waste of time. Archdeacon was as skeptical as the army about the Wrights' claims. In fact, he wrote an article for the magazine *Les Sports* in which he stated that the Wrights were "bluffing." Archdeacon strongly opposed striking a deal with the Wrights. It would be far better, he proposed, to pay a French consortium — made up of Ferber, himself, and others — a mere 200,000 francs; their combined efforts would soon produce an airplane comparable, or superior, to that of the Wrights.

It was a frustrating period for the Wrights; their various negotiations seemed to have come to a standstill. In an attempt to exert a little pressure, the brothers sent letters to the *Scientific American*, the Royal Aeronautical Society in Britain, the German journal *Illustrierte Aeronautische Mitteilungen*, and to *L'Aérophile*. In addition, they gave the letter to *L'Auto*, an influential daily paper — which promptly sent a reporter to Ohio.

Then Ferber committed an unfortunate error. In his zeal to support the Wrights, he released all the information he had on their accomplishments. Ill-advisedly, he included the brothers' comment about the Kaiser being truculent. Infuriated, the Wrights immediately lost all confidence in his ability to represent their interests.

Ferber, blissfully unaware of the Wrights' feelings, was still hoping to interest the French government in purchasing the Wright airplane. He contacted Frank S. Lahm, an American member of the Aéro-Club, whose brother-in-law, M.H. Weaver, lived in Mansfield, Ohio. Lahm, in turn, asked Weaver to find out what was going on in Dayton. Were the Wrights' claims justified? Were they really so far ahead of the rest of the world? After a trip to Dayton, Weaver cabled Lahm with the necessary confirmation. A follow-up letter appeared in *L'Auto*, *Les Sports*, and the Paris edition of the New York *Herald*.

Ferber used this good news at an Aéro-Club dinner in December to convince two of its members — Cartier, the well-known jeweler, and Desouches, a lawyer — that there was no risk in approaching the Wrights to assess their intentions. Cartier and Desouches introduced Ferber to Henri Letellier, a wealthy contractor and publisher of the Paris newspaper *Le Journal*. Letellier agreed to send his secretary, Arnold Fordyce, to the United States as a representative of a syndicate interested in obtaining a contract with the Wrights.

Ferber wired the brothers, asking that they meet Fordyce when he arrived in Dayton on December 28. It didn't take the brothers long to realize that he represented a group of businessmen, not government officials. The Wrights preferred to deal with governments, but that approach had achieved little to date, so they listened to what Fordyce had to say. He told them that Cartier et al.

EN AMÉRIQUE
Expériences d'un nouvel Aéroplane à Kitty-Hawk (Caroline du Nord)

(Above) International reports of the Wrights' Kitty Hawk flights appeared in such newspapers as France's Le petit Parisien *in January 1904, but received little public attention.*

planned to purchase the aircraft and present it as a gift to the French government. They would earn nothing but the gratitude of the nation.

By December 30, Wilbur and Orville had come to terms with the French syndicate. They agreed to divulge the full particulars of the design and construction of the Flyer — but to the French government, not to the businessmen. In this way, they reasoned, commercial exploitation could be avoided. A bond of $5,000 would be posted by February 5, 1906, and $200,000 would be deposited in a New York bank by April 5. The requirements for a demonstration remained unchanged, except that the brothers now promised to furnish an airplane capable of flying 160 kilometers with one person aboard. It was an encouraging development, but the stubborn Wrights still refused to show the aircraft without a contract.

With Fordyce's option in hand, Letellier contacted the minister of war, who agreed to serious negotiations with the Wrights. No doubt, the troubling international situation influenced his decision; many politicians now felt that war might break out at any time. And in the event of an armed conflict, the nation with the best aircraft would have an obvious advantage over all others. The minister dispatched a commission, led by Commandant Henri Bonel, chief of engineers for the French general staff. He was accompanied by Fordyce and two representatives from the French embassy, the military attaché, and a legal advisor.

Prior to the commission's arrival, Fordyce had exchanged telegrams with the Wrights in an effort to obtain a commitment to higher performance and to secure a longer period of exclusive rights for France. With scouting missions in mind, the French wanted an airplane capable of carrying two men to an altitude of three hundred meters. In early February, the Wrights cabled their agreement, at a price of 2,000,000 francs ($400,000) — or 1,200,000 francs, if France waived all priority rights. (The terms agreed upon earlier contained a clause restraining the Wrights from dealing with other countries for three months following fulfillment of the contract.)

The commission agonized over the matter of exclusive rights. France did not want Germany to have the Wright airplane. Then, unexpectedly, the political crisis cooled — and with it, the urgency to obtain the Wright airplane. The commission left Dayton with an agreement that was essentially the same as that negotiated with Fordyce four months earlier. However, the minister of war continued to press for the aircraft to be capable of higher altitudes, so the negotiations dragged on.

Although French aircraft design still lagged far behind the Americans', their engines were undoubtedly superior. One man was responsible: Léon Levavasseur, an excellent mechanical engineer and machinist who had built his reputation designing and constructing engines for speedboats. He had obtained financial support from Jules Gastembide, a wealthy manufacturer of electrical equipment whose daughter's name — Antoinette — identified their products. Levavasseur could supply engines weighing only four pounds per horsepower (half the weight of the Wrights' best) — and, by late 1906, as powerful as 50 HP. Levavasseur's engineering abilities served France well in those early days.

The hero of French aviation at that time was a Brazilian, Alberto Santos-Dumont. The son of a wealthy coffee planter, the diminutive adventurer had thrilled French spectators with his balloon and airship flights in the late 1890s. Usually seen in floppy white Panama hats and immensely tall collars, *le petit Santos* wore thick-soled shoes in an effort to add to his height of just over five feet. But what he lacked in stature he more than made up for in inventiveness and courage. In 1906, he produced his own airplane, the ungainly No. 14 bis. It looked like an untidy collection of box kites bolted together in no particular order. Murderously unstable in pitch, the ungainly craft tottered briefly into the air in September 1906, after lumbering along for nearly 1,000 feet. In October and November, the 14 bis successfully qualified for prizes amounting to 4,500 francs for flights of twenty-five and one hundred meters. As far as the French were concerned, Santos-Dumont was the world's greatest aviator. They hadn't seen the Wrights fly, so they had no basis for comparison.

Early in 1907, the Wrights entered into an arrangement with the Charles R. Flint Company of New York. Flint, a promoter and banker, would be the Wrights' business representative in Europe, where negotiations with the French government were still dragging on. Finally, in March 1908, a new French syndicate was formed, led by financier Lazare Weiller. It took only three weeks for the syndicate to agree to buy the Wrights' French patents and all rights to sell, manufacture, and license Wright airplanes in France.

At last, the seemingly endless negotiations were reaching a conclusion. It was agreed that once the Wrights had demonstrated their aircraft to everyone's satisfaction, a new company would be formed and the Wrights would train French pilots. No doubt heaving sighs of relief, Wilbur and Orville began to think about their forthcoming trip to France.

In 1907, an aviation enthusiast by the name of Henri Farman bought a Voisin aircraft. (Henri Voisin, inspired some years before by hearing Ferber lecture, had begun manufacturing aircraft for commercial use around this time.) British by birth, Farman had lived all his life in France and

(Left) The first hero of aviation in France was Brazilian Alberto Santos-Dumont, who thrilled French spectators with his inventive flying machines in the late 1890s and actually achieved flight in his No. 14 bis aircraft in 1906.

(Above) This sleek 1909 airplane was the work of the brilliant French mechanical engineer Léon Levavasseur, creator of the light and powerful Antoinette that gave France the lead in the design and manufacture of superior aviation engines.

knew only a few words of English. With his aircraft, he set out to win the Deutsch-Archdeacon prize for a closed-circuit flight of one kilometer. His performance was witnessed by the Wright brothers, who were in France at that time. They were not impressed, declaring that five years would elapse before any European would catch up with them.

But by January 1908, that gap seemed likely to close more rapidly than the brothers had predicted. Farman, like many aviators, was small of stature but bursting with enthusiasm and confidence; despite his lack of experience and the vagaries of his Voisin aircraft, he took off. The journal *American Aeronaut* reported breathlessly: "Gliding upwards to a height of four meters, it crosses the line between the posts . . . . Straight and true as an arrow, it makes for the starting point 500 meters distant, rising meantime by an adroit maneuver of the 'equilibrizer' to about 12 meters and remaining at that altitude. It rounds the far post 100 meters away from the path of its graceful curve. . . . The great bird is coming, gradually sinking to 4 meters until after recrossing the line, when the apparatus is let softly to the ground."

Farman was the man of the moment. In one minute and twenty-eight seconds, he had completed Europe's — and the world's — first official one-kilometer circuit. Two years before, the Wrights had flown thirty-nine times that distance near Dayton. But few in Europe knew or cared. As far as they were concerned, aeronautical history had been made precisely where it should have been made — in France. *The Times* of London agreed, amid a veritable avalanche of rhetoric: "Today has been an epoch-making event, that of the victory before official witnesses of human intelligence in its efforts to solve the problem which brought Icarus to grief, which tormented the brain of Leonardo da Vinci. Nothing of this kind has ever been accomplished before."

Still lacking the roll control of the Wright aircraft, Farman had flown the course in a wide, nearly flat turn,

literally skidding his way to victory. It was a fine accomplishment for an inexperienced aviator.

Ferber, the man who had to some extent started it all, noted in his journal: "This day marks the definitive conquest of the air." But there was little joy in his comment. He knew that he had been overtaken in the race to realize France's destiny in the air. His daughter recalled finding him in his den.

He told her, "I must remember that I will never make great flights. I had the idea, but others will make it happen." In February, he attended a dinner in Lyons with Farman and Voisin; but his role was toastmaster, not airman. The innovative captain of artillery had done much to stir up interest in aviation, but now his name was largely forgotten, just another pioneer whose contributions had become overshadowed by the progress of others.

By the early summer of 1908, there was an impressive array of hangars and workshops to be seen at Issy — and experimenters such as the Voisin brothers, Delagrange (who would soon take an attractive passenger, Thérèse Peltier, aloft, making her the first woman in the world to fly), Farman, Santos-Dumont, and Esnault-Pelterie were hard at work there. Even Ferdinand Ferber had a hangar. The captain still

when the well-known physiologist René Quinton became involved. Quinton's interest had been piqued during a trip to Egypt. In 1908, he enlisted Ferber's help in founding the National Aviation League, an organization devoted to all aspects of aeronautics except manufacturing.

Quinton was also a member of the "Forty-Five," a group of Parisian literary personalities who met once a month to

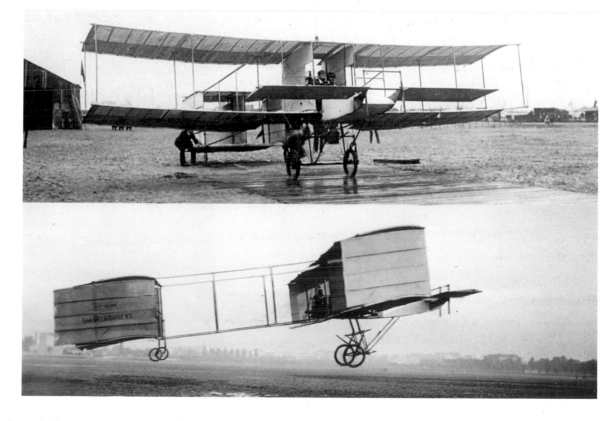

(Opposite) The Voisin brothers, who began manufacturing commercial aircraft in France in 1907. (Inset) Aviator Henri Farman, pictured here on his membership card for L'Aéro-Club de France, was the toast of France in 1909 — even though the Wright brothers had surpassed his feats a few years earlier in America. (Right) Two of Farman's aircraft designs, constructed at the Issy hangars in 1908, shortly after Wilbur flew in France for the first time.

hoped to make his mark in aviation. His No. 9 aircraft was similar to No. 8, but boasted a 50 HP Antoinette engine. In the spring of 1908, he managed a 770-meter flight. L'Eclair was impressed: "Each time the machine returns to earth, it is with surprising gentleness, and one has the impression of easy maneuverability." An odd comment, considering the aircraft was controllable only in pitch.

French interest in aeronautics received another boost

honor an individual of outstanding accomplishments in literature, arts, or the sciences. In May 1908, Quinton suggested that Ferber be honored at the June meeting. It was a great moment for the artillery captain who had done so much for French aviation. Ferber won over his audience "who applauded and acclaimed him." Following Ferber's successful address, Quinton established a prize of 10,000 francs for the first person to soar for five minutes without an engine.

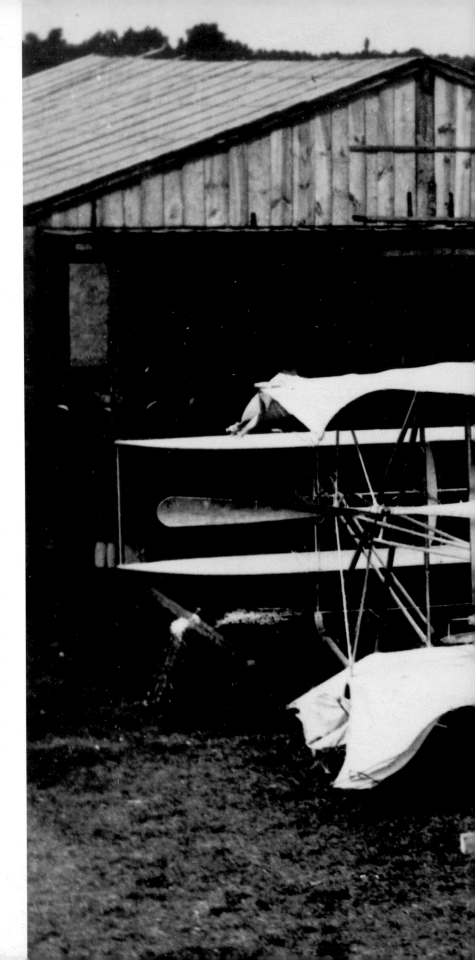

10
The GREAT White Bird

"We beheld the great white bird soar above the racecourse."

— French aviation writer
François Peyrey, 1908

The two French boys found it sidesplittingly funny. The tall *Americain* thought his airplane's shed was a hotel! He *lived* in there! Along with all the wood and fabric and wire, with the engine and all its dirt and smells. Was this the way airplane builders lived in America? Everyone said they were strange people on the other side of the ocean.

The boys snuggled down in their leafy hiding place as M. Wright emerged from the shed, a length of tubing in one hand, a wrench in the other. The boys smothered their giggles. He went walking by, not more than a meter from them, without seeing them. A lanky man with a hawklike profile, he invariably wore a deep frown. Had anyone seen him smile yet? None of the boys could recall such a sight. Building airplanes was evidently a deadly serious business for M. Wright.

(Right) A hundred miles southwest of Paris and far from the scrutiny of journalists, Wilbur and his assistants begin assembling the Flyer at Le Mans in early June 1908.

Now workmen began hauling the airplane out of its *hangar*, a great trembling insect of a thing with its sagging wings and its maze of wires. The American claimed his craft could fly better than Santos-Dumont's 14 bis, which was nonsense, for as everyone knew, Santos-Dumont was the greatest airman in the world.

Then they examined every part of the machine, tugging a wire here, a chain there. It looked flimsy. The boys were of the opinion that if by some miracle it did take to the air, it would fall to pieces, scattering its parts around Le Mans like some mechanical hailstorm.

The man called Wright looked as if he were dressed for the

(Left) Standing on a trestle, Wilbur supervises the raising of the upper wing. Despite his lack of French, the elder Wright brother still managed to communicate his instructions to the local assistants. (Opposite) Now seated at the controls — rather than lying flat, as he did at Kitty Hawk — Wilbur solemnly poses for the camera.

The American had been working on his airplane for weeks, taking the parts out of the packing cases in which it had journeyed from America, assembling it, repairing some parts that had been damaged during the trip. He had a handful of assistants, local men whose English was as painful as his French. But with gestures and sketches, they managed to make themselves understood to one another. During the testing, a pipe had torn loose from the engine, spraying the American with boiling water. A painful accident. But he didn't cry out or curse. And in fact he seemed far more vexed about the time the incident cost him than about the pain.

He and his assistants positioned the aircraft on its track.

city rather than for an aviation field. An odd one, all right. It was a warm day yet he wore a stiff collar and a business suit. He positioned himself in the small seat on the lower wing. He turned his cap back to front. A moment later, with a clattering and popping, the engine burst into life. And the propellers began to revolve. The enigmatic M. Wright took one more look about his creation, then he nodded to his assistants, and the weights in the derrick were released. Immediately, the great white bird began to move. The boys could hardly contain themselves. They watched open-mouthed as the craft trundled along its track. Then — miracle upon miracle! It flew! It climbed away from the field as easily as if a balloon were lifting it. But there

(*Above, left*) Wilbur makes a last-minute adjustment to the engine before taking his seat at the controls. (*Above, right*) As an enthusiastic group of volunteers tugs at the rope, the heavy weight that will fling the Flyer into the air rises slowly inside the derrick. During his public flights, Wilbur often asked local press and celebrities to lend a hand at the ropes. (*Below*) An astounded and appreciative crowd watches as Wilbur effortlessly maneuvers the Flyer through the darkening French sky.

was no balloon. Just a chattering motor and a tall man manipulating his levers. Easily, naturally, he banked the machine and circled the field. A minute later, he turned off the motor and the airplane sank to the ground, touching the grass with barely a bump. The crowd exploded in applause. They had never seen such a sight.

The man called Wright clambered out of the aircraft, acknowledging the congratulations of the onlookers. But he seemed ill at ease, as if anxious to get away from the throng.

Hiding behind the hedge, the boys still watched warily, as if monitoring the behavior of an unpredictable species. They dared not speak as M. Wright came striding back to the hangar, his mouth set in its usual thin line, as if he were about to attend an execution. A difficult man, M. Wright.

The boys held their breath as he came near.

Then something quite extraordinary happened. M. Wright stopped beside the boys' hiding place and looked down at them from his enormous height. Then he grinned. Actually grinned. And winked at them. After which he went on his way.

Wilbur had arrived in France in late May 1908. The visit had started out disastrously. On opening the packing cases containing the Flyer, Wilbur had found a considerable amount of damage. He blamed Orville, believing his brother had packed the various components poorly; later he realized that French Customs officials were the culprits. Weeks of work would be required to repair the aircraft. But one morsel of good news came Wilbur's way. An excellent — and inexpensive — flying field had been found at the Hunaudières racetrack in Le Mans, slightly more than a hundred miles southwest of Paris. Two public flying areas were also available nearer Paris: a section of Bagatelle, an estate in the wooded area of Bologne made famous by Santos-Dumont; and the field at Issy-les-Moulineaux, popularly known as "Issy," a sizable flat area intended originally for military parades. Wilbur liked the

Le Mans field, probably because it was far enough from Paris to discourage newspaper reporters. He set to work repairing the Flyer. He hired a few local workmen who spoke no English and didn't understand Wilbur's attempts at Ohio-accented French. Despite this, the workmen seemed to like the lanky American and the work went well. When his aircraft was at last ready, Wilbur decided to show the French a thing or two.

On Saturday, August 8, the crowds began to gather. Wilbur and his team spent most of the morning preparing the aircraft and its catapult mechanism. It was late afternoon when at last the Flyer's engine rattled into noisy life. Wilbur, dressed in a gray business suit, cap, and stiff white collar, looked as if he were about to spend the day in a bank; in fact, his natty attire caused a brief delay when his back-collar stud caught on a control wire and stopped the engine. The problem took only moments to fix, and the Flyer was soon trundling along its track, engine clattering, propellers revolving in their leisurely way. The machine lifted easily into the air.

"We beheld the great white bird soar above the racecourse," wrote leading French aviation writer François Peyrey. "We were able to follow easily each movement of the pilot, note his extraordinary proficiency in the flying business, perceive the curious warping of the wings in the process of circling, and the shifting of the rudders." One minute and forty-five seconds later, Wilbur returned to earth, with amazing "buoyancy and precision." The crowd exploded in applause. With a brief flight around the racetrack, Wilbur had silenced his critics. He was intensely relieved — although he did his best not to show it. No smiles. No signs of delight. The craggy, firm-jawed visage didn't change. It was typical Wilbur.

French airmen were astounded. Louis Blériot said, "Monsieur Wright has us all in his hands." Delagrange spoke for all French aviators when he admitted, "Well, we are

"I've seen him. Yes! I have today seen Wilbur Wright and his great white bird...." — Le Figaro

The Hero of the Hour

Before Wilbur flew at Les Hunaudières and Le Mans in August 1908, the Wrights had been called *"bluffeurs"* and *"bicycle peddlers"* by the dubious French. But his flights not only silenced the skeptics, they also caused an international sensation. *The Times* of London wrote that the Wrights deserved *"...conclusively, the first place in the history of flying machines."* French picture magazines (above) agreed, but the satirical journal *Le Rire* (right) depicted Wilbur as a mechanical vulture *"who flies as well as one of our hens."*

beaten." Every airman and designer took note of the Wrights' wing warping and understood its significance. The Americans had come up with the finishing touch, the final piece of the puzzle. Now the air had truly been conquered. The only sour note was contributed by Ernest Archdeacon, who declared the Flyer difficult to operate and its launching system cumbersome. "I consider our machines superior," he remarked. "In fact, they have wheels and can start wherever they may descend, without the help of rails." But no one was listening. Wilbur had become the hero of the hour, publicized in the press, lionized by the population. He even influenced fashion, his old green peaked cap being copied and sold by the thousand.

Meanwhile, in the United States, Orville prepared for the all-important U.S. Army tests. He arrived at Fort Myer, Virginia, on August 20. The parade ground had been selected for the aerial tests; it was an irregular tract of land west of the Arlington National Cemetery — 1,000 feet in length, 700 feet wide at the south end, and about 800 feet at the north. Although ideal for parades and sports, it was hardly large enough for flying. But the site had excellent facilities for repair and assembly. Fourteen stalwart army men were available to the Wrights and their assistants; they had previously assisted in the testing of Signal Corps Dirigible No. 1, built by Thomas Baldwin. The Wrights had lent Baldwin a hand in September 1906, when high winds had blown his airship out of the Dayton fairground. The corrugated iron shed used for the army's testing of Dirigible No. 1 was made available to Orville and his principal assistants, Charlie Furnas and Charlie Taylor.

Orville stayed at the St. James Hotel and, later, at the Cosmos Club, at the instigation of Albert Zahm, a leading

member of the Aero Club of America. Although relations between Zahm and the brothers would soon sour, they were cordial indeed in the summer of 1908. In fact, the two men were on such good terms that Zahm did his utmost to interest Orville in the "very handsome young ladies" in Washington — alas, without result.

Orville had competition, in the form of that will-o'-the-

Katharine and Orville at Fort Myer, Virginia, in September 1908.

wisp of the aeronautical world, Augustus Herring. Herring was convinced that a movable tail was the answer to all the problems associated with stability. He was never hesitant about releasing news of his latest triumphs, although no one ever saw the aircraft he described with such enthusiasm. The Wrights had long since lost patience with him. Herring had announced his intention of flying to Washington in his new machine, which, he declared, was automatically stable. Byron Newton of the New York *Herald* claimed to have seen the aircraft in Herring's shop on Broadway, although no one else did. Its arrival at Fort Myer was delayed again and again, purportedly because of an injury to Herring's finger.

Orville tested the Flyer's motor on August 27. Since the price the army paid would depend on performance, it was important to have the engine operating at peak efficiency. But during the first test, it stopped twice after running mere seconds. Then there was trouble with the bearings. After that, the recalcitrant motor began to skip. The problem? Poor-quality gasoline, Orville believed. Sight-feed oilers were installed on all outside bearings.

On Tuesday, September 1, the army tests began. First, portability. The tail and front rudder were unbolted and stowed between the wings. The machine was loaded onto an army combat wagon and towed out to the parade ground. On Thursday, September 3, word flashed quickly around Washington that Orville would fly that very afternoon. In no time, a sizable crowd had assembled, including members of various embassies and the president's son, twenty-year-old Theodore Roosevelt, Jr.

At 4:30 P.M., the Flyer was placed on the launching ramp. The motor wouldn't start. The crew attempted to revive it. With a bang, it came to life. Valves clattered, chains rattled, the big propellers began to revolve, and — wonder upon

wonder! — the Flyer surged forward. The crowd gasped. He was in the air! The crowd applauded wildly, although Orville could hear none of it. He was busy, turning east as he reached the south end of the field, soaring over Arlington Cemetery, passing over the spectators — some of whom ducked, although the Flyer had attained an altitude of some thirty-five feet by then.

Orville was on his second circuit when he made the mistake. The new control handles confused him and, in an instant, he was heading straight for a tent. He did the only thing possible and slammed the Flyer down, sending up a cloud of dust. He did minor damage to the skids and the front rudder braces. It was a less than spectacular perform-ance and the newspapers treated it accordingly. Most of the reporters had never seen an airplane fly; they had no way of knowing that they were witnessing a masterful display of maneuverability, except for the hasty landing. The New York *World*'s story talked of little more than the possibility of the "vessel," as the plane was termed, inadvertently flying into the crowd. Few understood that there was anything to choose between the simple, straight flight of Glenn Curtiss's June Bug and Orville's flight path with its repeated turns.

Orville was irked by the presence of Curtiss and Lieutenant Tom Selfridge, both members of the Aerial Experiment Association. Curtiss had talked at length with Orville and had examined the army Flyer carefully; he had then written

The Flyer rests on its track shortly before the first of the army aerial tests.

a long epistle to the chairman of the AEA, Alexander Graham Bell. Curtiss was contemptuous of the Flyer's engine — "crude and not exceptionally light." Orville took a strong dislike to Selfridge, who made a practice of pumping him for information whenever they met.

On September 9, Orville was at the field by 8 A.M., helping his crew position the Flyer on its track. The field was almost deserted when he took off. Fifty-seven and one-half minutes later, he landed — having established a new world record. It was just the beginning. He flew again that day, this time watched by a throng of Washingtonians. He flew for more than sixty-two minutes. The light was fading when Orville took off again, this time with Lieutenant Frank P. Lahm beside him. He flew for six minutes, breaking the record for passenger flight set on May 14 at Kill Devil Hills.

Over the next few days, Orville established several new records: an altitude of 200 feet; an endurance of one hour, fourteen minutes; and another altitude record of 310 feet. In four days, he set nine world records. Newspaper stories began to hint at a rivalry between the brothers, with the younger overtaking the older. Tongue in cheek, Wilbur admitted defeat in a letter to his brother: "The newspapers for several days have been full of the stories of your dandy flights and, whereas a week ago, I was a marvel of skill, now they do not hesitate to tell me that I am nothing but a 'dud' and that you are the only genuine skyscraper. Such is fame!" He was always ready with advice for his younger brother, concerning both flying and the niceties of etiquette, particularly in hotels, which some people at that time regarded as dens of iniquity. "Do not receive any one after 8 P.M. at night," Wilbur cautioned. At the time of this thoughtful counsel, Orville was thirty-seven years old!

Orville had taken Lieutenant Lahm and Major George Squier aloft in the Flyer. Now he felt obligated to do the same for Lieutenant Selfridge, although he distrusted the man. On the afternoon of Thursday, September 17, 1908, Selfridge took his place beside Orville. At 175 pounds, he was Orville's heaviest passenger to date, a fact emphasized by the Flyer's longer-than-usual takeoff run. The aircraft climbed rapidly, turning when it reached the field's boundary. Orville flew three circuits, from the army buildings in the west to Arlington Cemetery in the east. It was a good, enjoyable flight, and Orville began to make wider turns. It was then that he heard the tapping. He glanced down at his controls. All seemed to be well; nevertheless, Orville decided to land.

He didn't have time. Two loud bangs startled him. Spectators on the ground saw something fly from the airplane and spin earthward. Orville thought a chain might have broken. The aircraft swung to the right and headed for the trees lining the cemetery. Orville tried to correct. Nothing worked. Clutching the lever in his right hand, he could only watch as the disaster unfolded. The right wing rose. The Flyer now faced directly north. Orville worked the warping lever in an effort to level the wings. The aircraft immediately snapped into a near-vertical dive.

Orville heard Selfridge cry, "Oh! Oh!" He kept releasing the front rudder lever a little, then tugging at it. But he could see that the rudder (elevator) was bent to its limit, with the cloth bulging between the ribs. Some twenty-five feet from the ground, Orville felt the dive slackening. Maybe he would pull her out in time. Maybe. . . .

It was not to be. The wings began to fold, unable to take such punishment. The structure collapsed, the fabric ripping and fluttering like a flag. An instant later, the aircraft hit the

119

ground. The engine tore loose and thudded into the earth. Dust exploded like the burst of a cannon shell. For an endless moment, the Flyer and its occupants were invisible. The crowd was frozen. No one moved. Then, like a motion picture come to life, everyone leapt into action. Running, pointing, yelling. Automobile horns honked. Horses whinnied, frightened by the strange goings-on.

Slowly, as if reluctant to reveal the scene, the dust cleared. The wreckage lay in awful disarray. Wings twisted and broken. Skids reduced to matchwood. The two occupants lay still, pinned by the remains of the upper wing.

The rescuers lifted Orville and laid him on the grass. He was moaning softly. Selfridge's khaki uniform was bloodstained and ripped. He had a six-inch gash in his head. He made no sound as they carried his inert form from the wreckage.

A Dr. Watters from New York attended to Orville while three army surgeons who had been watching the flight from a car hurried to Selfridge's side. Convinced that Orville had died, Charlie Taylor broke down and burst into tears. Only when Dr. Watters assured him that the younger Wright's chances for a complete recovery were good, could he pull himself together.

That evening, the surgeons announced that Orville had suffered a fracture of the left thigh, several broken ribs, and serious scalp wounds. He had been lucky. The same couldn't be said for Tom Selfridge. He had suffered a fracture at the base of the skull. The doctors were still operating on him when he died shortly after 8 P.M. without regaining consciousness. Selfridge gained the melancholy distinction of becoming the first person to die in the crash of a powered airplane.

In France, Wilbur was about to take off on yet another demonstration flight when the cablegram — *le papier bleu* — arrived. It said that the Flyer had crashed on the Fort Myer parade ground. Selfridge had been killed; Orville was

The air is still thick with dust at the crash site as stunned bystanders struggle with the mangled wings of the Flyer. Luckily, several doctors had been watching the flight from a car and they hurried across the field to attend to the badly wounded passenger and pilot.

(Left) Selfridge, seen falling from the plane in this wildly stylized depiction of the crash, had the unhappy distinction of being the first fatality in a powered aircraft. (Right) A close-up view of some of the structural damage the Flyer sustained as a result of the crash.

injured. The cable didn't say how badly. A second cable arrived later in the day. Orville would recover. Wilbur breathed again.

The cause of the fatal accident was a faulty propeller. An eighteen-inch split had been discovered during servicing. As was the custom, the problem had been fixed by nailing the split together and gluing cloth over the damage. It was the standard remedy. But then, a longitudinal crack developed in one blade. During Orville's flight, the blade broke — it was the object seen spinning from the Flyer moments before the crash. The loss of the blade set up a violent vibration. This loosened a stay wire connected to the rudder, which was so severely tilted out of the vertical that it acted as an elevator, making the aircraft viciously uncontrollable.

Wilbur's feelings were made clear in a letter to Katharine: "I cannot help thinking over and over again, 'If I had been there, it would not have happened.' The worry over leaving Orville alone to undertake those trials was one of the chief things in almost breaking me down a few weeks ago and as soon as I heard reassuring news from America I was well again. A half dozen times I was on the point of telling Berg

that I was going to America in spite of everything. It was not right to leave Orville to undertake such a task alone."

Orville remained in the hospital for six weeks. His thigh had knitted, although his left leg would always be an eighth of an inch shorter than his right and he would suffer almost constant pain.

Early in September, Alexander Graham Bell, Douglas McCurdy, and Casey Baldwin came to pay their respects at the Fort Myer hospital. Forbidden by Orville's doctor to see the patient, they left cards, after which they set out on foot for Arlington National Cemetery to view Selfridge's casket. On the way, they looked in the shed where the remains of the army Flyer had been placed, awaiting return to Dayton. To Orville's subsequent displeasure, they were permitted by the guard in charge to examine the wreckage at their leisure.

Several months later, Wilbur wrote to Chanute describing the accident and how it happened: "One blade of the right propeller developed a longitudinal crack which permitted the blade to flatten out and lose its pushing power. The opposite blade not being balanced by an equal pressure on the injured blade put strains on its axle and its supports, which permitted it to swing forward and sidewise a little farther than the normal position and at the same time set up a strong vibration. This brought the uninjured blade in contact with the upper stay wire to the tail and tore it loose, the end of the wire wrapping around the end of the blade and breaking it off. The blade which broke off was not the one which originated the trouble."

Meanwhile, the ever-active Augustus Herring delivered what he claimed was his army airplane. According to most reports, it was carried in a suitcase. In the presence of the Aeronautical Board, Herring assembled what he called a center section of a biplane. It was controlled in flight, Herring explained, by twisting the struts beside the pilot's seat. The Board granted Herring a third monthly extension, to mid-November, to enable him to complete the machine. Herring had earned a reputation as a publicity-hungry individual. Now he was strangely reserved, refusing to let reporters see what was inside his case. This proved unfortunate for him, as the papers had their revenge: "The Herring airship is packed in a suitcase," declared the New York *Herald*. "This is the safe way to use it." On the other hand, *Harper's Weekly* took Herring seriously, stating, "The Aeronautical Board of the United States Army assembled at Fort Myer is reported to be convinced that this invention has positively and finally solved the question of flight by man." The gullible reporter who interviewed Herring had no doubts concerning his subject's probity. "His gaze meets yours with the utmost frankness, and yet it is impossible to escape the belief that the intelligence back of those eyes is busy with something else even while the man gives candid answers to every question."

Flyer the dog

Candid answers? Herring couldn't even tell the truth about his age. He was forty-three but he claimed to be thirty-five. He waxed eloquent about his aircraft, saying that it was a mere one-fourth the size of the Wright airplane, with its wing in sections so that its size might be varied depending on the load to be carried. The Wright Flyer could carry only two men; Herring's too-good-to-be-true machine could carry up to a dozen. No catapult was needed to propel it into the air. A run of five or ten feet would suffice. No one ever saw the aircraft fly. No one even saw it assembled. Yet Herring claimed that the machine was tested on October 28, near Hempstead, Long Island. The only witness? A neighbor's boy — "or someone else," he testified vaguely in court several years later.

Orville was discharged from the Fort Myer hospital on October 31 and left that night for Dayton with Katharine, who had helped nurse him back to health. Bishop Wright noted: "His mind is as good as ever and his body promises to be in due time." By mid-November, Orville was up and about, hobbling on crutches and working with Katharine to answer some of the five hundred letters from well-wishers.

In France, Wilbur continued to demonstrate the Flyer, often delighting the reporters who haunted the camp near Le Mans by enlisting them as airfield laborers, having them haul the Flyer in and out of its shed. Wilbur had become the most celebrated personality of the day.

But despite their affection, the French found Wilbur a puzzle. The man was totally indifferent to the finer things in life. He lived in the shed with the Flyer, in company with an ugly but affectionate mongrel dog also named Flyer. He appeared not to care about the inadequacies of his quarters

Mad about Wilbur

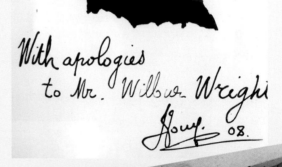

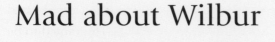

CHAPEAU EXTRA LÉGER

With apologies to Mr. Wilbur Wright

Wilbur became one of the first celebrities of the new century — "the birdman," the "poet of flight," the victor "o'er the realms of the air." But the French also viewed the ascetic older Wright brother as an enigma. "Has he a heart? Has he loved?" asked one magazine. Another cast him — utterly against type — as a Parisian *apache* (below), with drooping cigarette and admiring

female by his side. His image appeared on ads for "Extra-light hats" (above), and copies of his distinctive green cloth cap — known as "Veelburs" — were sold all over France. (Above right and right) Sketches of Wilbur and postcards of his flights at Le Mans were popular souvenirs of the day.

or their lack of privacy. He was never safe from prying eyes. One woman used a gimlet to bore a hole through the wooden wall so that she might watch him. Wilbur said he couldn't take a bath without a hundred or so citizens keeping an eye on him. Every level of French society adored him. Kings and princes, soldiers and laborers; he was a hero to all. The young Spanish painter, Pablo Picasso, nicknamed a friend "Vilbare."

Crowds arrived daily to watch him fly. They traveled to the field by what was called the Le Mans-Auvours Aeroplane Bus Service — a fleet of local taxis whose owners had never had it so good. The shops were full of souvenir postcards featuring caricatures of the American's hawklike features. He received an impossibly generous number of invitations to meals and various social functions. Invited to the Aéro-Club de la Sarthe, he made a speech memorable for its brevity: "I know of only one bird, the parrot, that talks, and it can't fly very high."

Wilbur took up some sixty passengers at Camp d'Auvours. His first was the portly Léon Bollée. The fact that the Flyer was capable of lifting the 240-pound Bollée was proof of the airplane's efficiency. Mrs. Hart O. Berg, wife of the Wrights' European agent, became one of the first women to fly. Before takeoff, she fastened a cord about her ankles, lest her gown be blown about by the wind. After her flight, Mrs. Berg hobbled a few steps before removing the cord. A fashion designer is said to have seen her; thus was born the hobble-skirt fad.

Part of the contract between the Wrights and the French government called for the training of three French pilots to fly the aircraft. Training was supposed to start at the end of

October, but the weather didn't cooperate. The weeks passed and Wilbur grew tired of Camp d'Auvours. He wanted to be home for Christmas, but there seemed little chance now of the job being completed in time. He asked his family to join him in Europe; unfortunately, Bishop Wright, now eighty, was not up to the trip. Katharine decided to leave her teaching job at Steele High once more and accompany Orville to

(Left) Mrs. Hart O. Berg, posing here with Flyer, was one of the first women to fly. (Right) At 240 pounds, French automobile pioneer Léon Bollée, right, was among the heaviest passengers to ride in the Flyer with Wilbur.

Europe so that the two inseparables would be together.

In the meantime, Wilbur continued to live in the airplane hangar with the dog Flyer. Heat was provided by a small stove. In November, he traveled to Paris to be awarded various honors. Typically, it troubled rather than pleased him. The papers were full of him and his airplane. Wasn't it inevitable that there would be a backlash? Any day now, Wilbur was sure, the French would tire of him. But his concerns were groundless. The French continued to adore and admire him.

French aviators were doing their best to catch up to "Vilbare," adding various means of lateral control to their machines to make them as efficient as the Wright Flyer. Soon, the benefits became apparent. On October 30, Henri Farman made the first cross-country flight in history, covering twenty-seven kilometers from Camp de Chalons to Reims in twenty minutes.

Some Frenchmen salved national pride by clinging tenaciously to the belief that Clément Ader had been the first to fly a powered aircraft, half a dozen years before the Wrights. Others claimed that Santos-Dumont's 1906 flight in the dreadful 14 bis was the first in history. Perhaps such claims were inevitable.

In December 1908, the largest aeronautical exposition held to date opened in Paris at the Grand Palais. Ader's Avion was given pride of place between the two principal stairways leading to the exhibition area. Nationalistic fervor prompted many an ill-judged statement. The Aéro-Club de France kept stirring up the patriotic pot. They prevented Wilbur from competing in the club's 2,500-franc, twenty-five-meter altitude prize by stipulating that the winning craft must take off under its own power without using falling weights to jog it into motion. Although the Flyer did not compete, Wilbur demonstrated that he could have won the prize anyway; he extended the length of the takeoff track and took off without the weights.

In October, the London *Daily Mail* had offered a prize of £1,000 ($5,000) for the first flight across the English Channel. Wilbur was tempted (the *Mail* offered him money just to enter), but Orville cautioned him: "I do not like the idea of your attempting a channel flight when I am not present. I haven't much faith in your motor running. You seem to have more trouble with the engine than I do."

Wilbur tended to agree and confined his efforts to winning the Michelin Cup for the longest flight of the year. He would have liked to return to Dayton for Christmas but he was aware that several others were also in the running for the Michelin. On December 18, Wilbur took off at about 10 A.M. and flew the course in the face of strong winds and blowing snow. After nearly two hours, he had to land because of a clogged oil line — but not before he had covered close to one hundred kilometers. Later that same day, Wilbur took off again in an attempt to win the 1,000-franc Prix de la Hauteur. A captive balloon marked the height to be attained. He reached it with ease, attaining an altitude of 350 feet, the highest anyone had ever been in an airplane.

On the last day of the year, Wilbur took off, intending to set a two-hour endurance record. A broken fuel line brought him down after forty-two minutes. He took to the air again, winging his way around the triangular course. In an unpleasant downpour of sleet and rain, he plowed on for two hours and twenty minutes. The French government awarded the brothers the Legion of Honor. A few days later, Wilbur went to Paris to greet Orville and Katharine. The next day, Wilbur set off for Pau in the south of France to train three French pilots — and Orville and Katharine narrowly missed death when they were involved in a collision between two trains. Miraculously, neither was hurt.

The city of Pau had gone to a lot of trouble and expense to lure Wilbur, offering him a mile-square flying field at Pont-Long, a few miles from town. The hangar that would accommodate the Flyer had a workshop for repairs, and doors large enough for the airplane to be trundled in and out of the hangar with both tail frame and front rudder attached. As had been his custom at Le Mans, Wilbur slept at the field but in quarters infinitely superior to those in the north. A French chef had been selected by the mayor to provide Wilbur's meals, and a special telephone line was installed, connecting the field with Pau, where Orville and Katharine were staying at the luxurious Hotel Gassion, free of charge.

Wilbur's three students were Paul Tissandier, Captain Paul Lucas-Girardville, and Count Charles de Lambert. They learned to operate the horizontal front rudder — the elevator

A commemorative postcard from the French town of Pau, where Wilbur trained his French pilots.

— first, then the warping and rudder control stick between the seats. Wilbur rode beside each student, his hands on his knees, ready to take over in case of trouble. There was none. The three pupils completed their training by March 19, dismaying the anti-Wright clique in France that maintained the operation of the Flyer was too complex.

The city profited hugely from the presence of the Wrights. Kings and politicians, generals and lords; they all came to Pau to see the remarkable "Vilbare." And they delighted in being photographed either in the airplane or tugging on the rope that hauled the hefty collection of weights up the starting derrick. King Alfonso of Spain wanted to take a flight with Wilbur. His queen persuaded him to remain on the ground. Edward, the portly King of England, needed no persuasion; he had no intention of trusting his hefty frame to anything as fragile as the Flyer. The fashionable visitors to Pau found the three Wrights fascinating, and none more so than the enigmatic Wilbur. Most reporters described his features as "hawklike," an appropriate description for the world's premier aviator. Wilbur's habit of wearing a business suit and shirt and

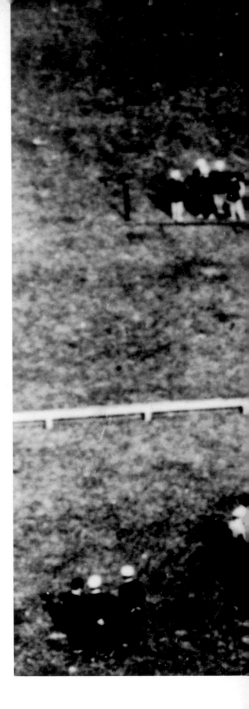

(Left) Celebrities, politicians, and royalty flocked to Pau to meet the legendary Wilbur Wright. (Top) Press baron Lord Northcliffe, in his fur coat, joins other enthusiastic "assistants" in hoisting the weight that will catapult the Flyer into the air. (Bottom) King Alfonso of Spain, left, listens attentively as Wilbur describes the operations of the Flyer. (Right) An aerial shot of Centocelle, outside Rome, where the Wrights trained a pilot to fly the plane they had sold to the Italian government.

collar when he flew contrasted with the European flyers who favored flamboyant scarves and natty leathers.

One thing about the Wrights flummoxed the journalists: the brothers' bewildering lack of interest in the opposite sex. One newspaper claimed that a French army officer was taking Wilbur to court for seducing his wife and living with her for two weeks in a Le Mans hotel. The story was a total fabrication. The Wrights appeared to have no interests apart from aviation and their family.

They soon had to journey to Rome to deliver a Flyer and train a pilot. In late March, Wilbur and Hart Berg traveled to the Italian capital. On April 2, they were presented to King Victor Emmanuel. Wilbur was fascinated by the king's diminutive proportions. When the monarch sat down, his feet dangled about a foot from the floor.

Wilbur flew from a field named Centocelle. A shed had

been erected for the Flyer; Wilbur slept in a local cottage and usually ate with the officers at the nearby fort. His pupil pilot was Lieutenant Mario Calderara of the Italian Navy. The instruction proceeded satisfactorily and the three Wrights left Rome at the end of April, calling in at Le Mans for a farewell banquet — which they left, loaded down with the city's coat of arms on a gold plaque, as well as medals and a bronze statuette commissioned by the Aéro-Club de la Sarthe.

In England, they picked up two more medals; seven days later, they arrived back in the United States, far better known than when they'd departed. In New York, they attended a luncheon given by the Aero Club of America, after which they boarded the train for Dayton. Their hopes for a quiet family reunion were quickly dashed. As if to make up for the lack of interest that followed the 1903 flight, the entire city came out to greet them. A carriage drawn by four white horses took them from the depot, accompanied by a marching band playing "Home, Sweet Home." On Hawthorn Street, Chinese lanterns were strung between the elms and poplars; the Wright house was hardly recognizable under its mantle of flags and banners.

Then it was off to Washington to receive gold medals from the Aero Club of America, presented by President William Howard Taft himself — after which, the city of Dayton decided

To which a member of the cast responded: "They are no other than two of Dayton's illustrious sons coming home from foreign triumphs with the greatest invention of the age." Not the snappiest dialogue ever, but no one minded.

In response, the taciturn Wilbur rose and said, "Thank you, gentlemen." And sat down.

By 4 P.M., the festivities were over and the two imperturbable brothers returned to their cycle shop. At 9 P.M., the city

(Above) During May and June of 1909, the dignitaries and citizens of Dayton paid tribute to their native sons. Thousands waited at the train station (left) to greet their heroes. (Right) Marching bands, festive banners, and a spectacular evening fireworks display marked the auspicious occasion. (Opposite) Crowds of well-wishers in front of the Wright home dispelled any hopes Wilbur and Orville had of a quiet homecoming.

to welcome the boys home with a full-scale civic celebration. In mid-June, schools and most businesses closed down. A carriage trundled along Hawthorn Street and picked up the city's favorite sons. In Van Cleve Park, a man dressed as Jonathan Dayton stepped from a boat in the river surrounded by heralds and colonial soldiers. According to the press, the man portraying Dayton declaimed: "Methinks I see two great objects like gigantic birds coming from the eastward as if riding on the wings of the morning! What manner of birds can these be?"

seemed to explode as fireworks "painted" the portraits of Wilbur and Orville in the sky. The celebration involved the entire city, including all fifteen members of the Wright family, plus a thousand children dressed in red, white, and blue, forming an American flag, after which they rendered a selection of patriotic songs. Wilbur and Orville received Congressional Medals of Honor. The state governor awarded them with medals; the mayor of Dayton presented diamond-studded medals. Typically, the Wrights found it all rather tiresome.

Fort Myer

"We have been very busy on a machine for Fort Myer and as we are interrupted very much the work goes slower than we could wish...."

— Wilbur Wright to Octave Chanute, June 6, 1909

After the hullabaloo at Dayton, Fort Myer, Virginia, seemed staid and sober. The new Flyer was to undergo tests before representatives of the government and the U.S. Army. Orville would fly the airplane, while Wilbur would ensure that the aircraft was properly assembled and maintained. Charlie Taylor would assist him.

On June 28, 1909, a sizable crowd of onlookers — most of them senators and congressmen — had journeyed in vain to Fort Myer. The wind had strengthened and the Wrights decided not to fly. The newspapers immediately accused the brothers of snubbing their distinguished guests. As evening approached on Tuesday, the 29th of June, Orville attempted to take off but couldn't maintain flying speed after leaving the ramp. The right wing hit the ground and the Flyer swung to a sudden stop. Damage was negligible. Forty minutes later, Orville clattered along the ramp for the second time. He rose. Eight seconds later, he was down again.

Wilbur diagnosed the problem as improper balance.

(Opposite) Flag in hand, Wilbur goes over last-minute details before Orville, right, and Lieutenant Ben Foulois depart for the U.S. Army trials' compulsory two-person, cross-country flight. (Above) The new Flyer sits ready on the ramp at Fort Myer.

Eighteen pounds of iron bars were fastened to the horizontal front rudder, but the Flyer still seemed strangely reluctant to fly. It skidded for some two hundred feet across the parade ground without lifting. Was the problem with the spark lever? On every takeoff, it had slipped back because of lack of friction. Undoubtedly, the steamy summer heat had contributed to the Flyer's poor performance. With evening closing in, Orville took off yet again, and returned after a single circuit of the field. That was enough for one day. On Wednesday morning, the crew added several feet to the takeoff ramp. Orville got into the air, briefly, but broke a skid on landing. It was a less than sterling performance and must have prompted a few doubts among the generals.

On the evening of Friday, July 2, Orville took off and circled for eight minutes. Then his motor stopped. He glided down to land but hit a small tree at the south end of the parade ground. The Flyer dropped heavily to the ground, shaking Orville without injuring him.

Another week went by while repairs were made. By July 9, the Flyer was ready but high winds precluded flying. Then the motor started giving trouble. After which, the skids gave trouble. It began to look as if the Flyer would never perform satisfactorily. But as abruptly as it had arrived, the spell of bad luck vanished. Orville flew for almost seventeen minutes, passing over the cavalry stables and the nearby powerhouse. The flights attracted enormous attention, as immense numbers of citizens swarmed across the Potomac to see the extraordinary Wright airplane that everyone was talking about.

On Monday, July 26, President Taft arrived with Vice President James Sherman to inspect the Flyer. The next day, Orville embarked on the first of the tests required by the Signal Corps contract. It was to be a two-man flight of at least one hour and it would have to be completed in less than ideal conditions. Black clouds threatened, while a brisk wind battered the trees. Lieutenant Lahm settled into the passenger's seat, no doubt aware that Tom Selfridge had started

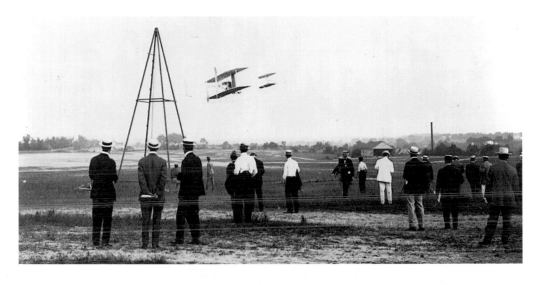

(Opposite) Orville flies gracefully over Arlington National Cemetery during the final days of the army trials. (Above) As officials and spectators look on, Orville maneuvers the Flyer past the starting tower on one of the trial flights.

his fatal last flight in just the same way. Orville took off moments after the presidential automobile had arrived. An hour later, he landed, having satisfied that part of the test.

The contract also called for a ten-mile cross-country flight with two men aboard. This was to be the first cross-country flight in the United States (Farman had successfully completed the world's first in 1908). Orville decided on a round-trip flight to Alexandria, five miles away. Weight was critical in the underpowered Flyer. Orville had sensibly selected Lieutenant Ben Foulois, who, at 5 feet, 1 inch, weighed only 126 pounds;

Blériot Conquers the English Channel

Le Petit Journal

LA TRAVERSÉE DU PAS-DE-CALAIS EN AÉROPLANE
Blériot atterrit sur la falaise de Douvres

AS M. FONTAINE SAW IT: M. BLÉRIOT'S LANDING AT DOVER.

Eccentric French aviator Louis Blériot had already designed, built, and flown more than a dozen aircraft when he took off on July 25, 1909, in his Blériot XI monoplane — determined to win the £1,000 prize for flying across the English Channel. The Frenchman carried no compass, it was a cloudy day, and the wind started blowing him to the north. Coming across three ships, he followed them, gambling that they were headed for Dover — and, sure enough, the English city's famed white cliffs soon came into sight. In thirty-seven minutes, Blériot had become the new hero of the skies.

(Left) Louis Blériot approaches the coastline of Dover in the last minutes of his historic flight across the English Channel. The dapper French aviator (inset, left) became the newest aviation celebrity, and French newspapers (above) were quick to immortalize the moment for the glory of France.

besides, Foulois had some experience at map reading so he would be able to assist in finding the checkpoints.

The Flyer took off at six o'clock on the evening of Friday, July 30. Orville circled the parade ground twice, then roared over the starting line. Wilbur and Foulois, as well as members of the Aeronautical Board, started their stopwatches.

Orville flew at an altitude of a little over a hundred feet, constantly correcting as a southwesterly wind kept blowing the Flyer off course. At times, the aircraft sagged in the summer downdrafts but Orville calmly worked the controls to regain altitude. His competence impressed Foulois, who would become a skilled pilot himself and would eventually command the U.S. Army Air Corps.

When the Flyer was spotted approaching Fort Myer on its return journey, the crowd went wild with delight. The Wrights had done it! The U.S. War Department paid them $30,000 for the aircraft.

An important flight took place in Europe at this time. Louis Blériot, the indestructible French aviator who had made a fortune in the automobile accessory business, was recovering from burns suffered during an endurance trial, when the asbestos covering the exhaust pipe had burned away and exposed the glowing pipe to Blériot's foot. Now, he walked with the aid of crutches. His aircraft, the Blériot XI, was a monoplane with only 150 square feet of wing area, powered by a three-cylinder 25 HP motor built by an Italian named Alessandro Anzani. It was a crude, messy engine but a remarkably reliable one, making it an appealing choice for a shot at the Channel crossing.

In fact, according to Blériot, the Anzani didn't miss a beat. He landed near Dover Castle, breaking his landing gear in the process — a minor incident, by his standards. The thirty-eight-kilometer flight had taken thirty-seven minutes. Blériot was the new hero of the air. When his monoplane was displayed at Selfridge's department store in London,

some 120,000 people lined up for a close look. Returning to France, Blériot was received like Napoleon. His monoplane was trundled through the streets of Paris for all to see and admire, a triumphal aerial chariot.

Blériot's participation in the Reims air show — the *Grande Semaine d'Aviation de la Champagne* — guaranteed the show's success. The leading champagne houses put up 200,000 francs ($40,000) in prizes for speed, distance, and altitude. The most prestigious award was the *Coupe Internationale d'Aviation*, a silver trophy that in its very flamboyance seemed to typify its donor, the ebullient James Gordon Bennett, publisher of the New York *Herald*.

Entries included Voisins, Blériots, Antoinettes, Henri Farmans, and six Wrights owned by Frenchmen. The Wrights themselves did not participate. "I am only interested in building and selling airplanes," Wilbur declared frostily. "Let others amuse themselves with races if they want to."

American hopes rested on that taciturn thirty-year-old from the wine country of upstate New York, Glenn Curtiss. He was already involved in heated battle with the Wrights, having run afoul of them and their patents on wing warping. The Wrights were of the opinion that anyone who built and flew an aircraft should pay them a royalty; their tactics won them few friends. The legal battles would drag on for years, generating fervid hatreds and blunting the progress of aviation in the United States. (In early 1914, Curtiss attempted to invalidate the Wright patent by assisting in the reconstruction of the hapless Langley Aerodrome; his aim was to be able to state that the Wrights weren't the first to fly. Although the much-modified Aerodrome did manage a successful, if brief, flight over Keuka Lake in upstate New York on May 28, 1914, the flight had little impact on the legal battles, which ended in the Wrights' favor.)

Curtiss won the speed prize at Reims, flashing over the finish line at an average speed of 47.65 MPH, in his Reims

"I do not compete for trophies. . . ."

— Wilbur Wright to journalist
Heinrich Adams, 1909

Racer with its 50 HP water-cooled V-8 motor. He narrowly edged out Blériot, who had been confident of victory. Henri Farman won the distance prize — 112 miles at an average speed of 45 MPH — and Hubert Latham (who might have beaten Blériot across the Channel had his engine not quit within sight of the English coast) won the prize for altitude, soaring up to 508 feet.

Perhaps the most remarkable fact about the great Reims meet was that not a single aviator lost his life — an amazing achievement, considering the incredible lack of experience among most of the pilots. One, Étienne Bunau-Varilla, had just graduated from high school and his well-to-do father had given him an airplane as a reward. The enthusiastic pupil immediately set to work learning to fly it just days before the show began. Another, a Monsieur Ruchonnet, had begun flight training the weekend before the meet.

Orville went to Germany to demonstrate the Flyer. It was a highly successful visit; Orville took Crown Prince Friedrich Wilhelm for a fifteen-minute flight, after which he was presented with a diamond-and-ruby stickpin. Orville also broke Latham's altitude record, climbing to about 1,600 feet.

Wilbur had been busy, too. At the Hudson-Fulton Celebration, commemorating the 300th anniversary of Henry Hudson's exploration of the Hudson River in the *Half Moon*, as well as the 102nd anniversary of Robert Fulton's journey in the *Clermont*, he was to fly a distance of ten miles or one hour in duration. Glenn Curtiss was also scheduled to appear, flying over the Hudson from Governors Island in Upper New York Bay to Grant's Tomb on Riverside Drive in Upper Manhattan. Two hangars had been erected on the sand flats at Governors Island for the Wright and Curtiss aircraft.

Although the Wright brothers preferred not to take part in the prestigious Reims air show personally, six of their airplanes, including the one at left piloted by Eugène Lefebvre, were entered by their French owners.

139

The ship bringing Curtiss and his aircraft back from Europe docked on September 21. The next morning, Curtiss took the ferry to Governors Island. He stopped at the Wright hangar and exchanged cordial greetings with Wilbur. No one witnessing the meeting would have suspected that there was any ill feeling between the two.

Augustus Herring, always on the lookout for opportunities to make a dollar, arranged for Wanamaker's, the New York department store, to display Curtiss's Reims Racer for a fee of $5,000. Since the Racer was thus engaged, Curtiss had to practice for the show with an untried aircraft powered by a 24 HP engine.

On October 4, Wilbur took off from Governors Island with an unusual addition between the landing skids: a canoe. Since the day's program called for a lengthy flight over water, he felt the canoe was a worthy addition to his equipment. Should he come down in the water, he felt reasonably certain that the canoe would support him and the Flyer until rescuers arrived.

From Governors Island, he turned to fly northward up the Hudson to Grant's Tomb, after which he turned back and flew south, back to the island, where he landed without having had to put the canoe to use. Wilbur's journey up the Hudson made headlines, having been witnessed by what was undoubtedly the single largest audience ever to see a man fly. It was possibly the high point of the Wrights' flying careers. The truth was, the Europeans were catching up.

(Right) Wilbur's majestic flight up the Hudson was immortalized in this painting by William S. Phillips. The flight, a tribute to two of America's most famous explorers, also marked the climax of the Wright brothers' successes as aviation pioneers. (Above) Wilbur's commemorative lapel ribbon from the Hudson-Fulton Celebration.

"It was an interesting trip and at times rather exciting."

— Wilbur Wright, describing to his father his flight from Governors Island to Grant's Tomb on October 4, 1909

SPECTATOR Sport

"There is no sport equal to that which aviators enjoy while being carried through the air on great white wings."

— Wilbur Wright, 1905

The promotional poster (left) and postcards (right) show how quickly aviators on both sides of the Atlantic joined the lucrative air-show circuit, thrilling paying audiences with their feats of airborne daring. (Opposite) The hangar at the Wrights' flying school in Montgomery, Alabama, festooned with local advertising.

The success of the Reims meet ushered other promoters into the field. Aviation had become a spectator sport. And a hugely profitable one. Initially, the mere sight of an airplane in flight was enough to thrill the crowds, but that soon changed. Before long, stunts of increasing daring were needed to draw a crowd — and proven attractions were rewarded accordingly. Exhibition pilots could earn up to $1,000 a day at a time when a family with an income of $500 a year considered itself fortunate.

To promote and sell their aircraft, the Wright brothers decided reluctantly to get involved in this lucrative but dangerous activity. In March of 1910, they recruited a cadre of pilots and opened a flying school in Montgomery, Alabama, where the winter weather was mild enough for training. Arch Hoxsey was the best known of the Wright pilots, with Ralph Johnstone, a trick bicycle rider and former circus clown, a close rival. Frank Coffyn, a young New Yorker from a banking family, was another. Coffyn thought highly of the Wright brothers, remembering Wilbur as a "very thoughtful and wonderful character." Orville taught Coffyn the basics in about an

hour and a half, then Walter Brookins took over and completed Coffyn's instruction.

Glenn Curtiss liked the exhibition business, too, and he also formed a team of pilots. His first was a former Harvard student, Charles Willard; his second, Charles "Daredevil" Hamilton, was a red-haired, jug-eared flier who would achieve considerable fame — and would, improbably, die in bed of tuberculosis at age twenty-eight, after surviving no fewer than sixty-three crashes.

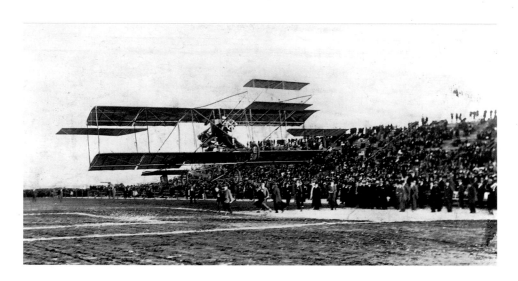

They were a colorful lot, those early exhibition pilots. Curtiss hired Beckwith Havens, a clean-cut young automobile salesman who could have posed for the famous Arrow collar advertisements. He recalled the dangers posed by wind: "When it was blowing hard, nobody wanted to fly if they could help it, but the crowd would demand that you go up. The program said you were going to fly at two-thirty. Well, maybe the wind was blowing pretty hard. You were always watching the wind, you know — watching smoke, watching flags, laundry on the line, and everything. I still do it."

In Enid, Oklahoma, Havens ran into a skeptical crowd who doubted that Havens could fly. A strong wind was blowing and

Havens tried to stall, knowing that the wind would die down toward sundown: "To kill time, and also to see if there were any gopher holes that might trip me up, I started walking away from the grandstand. Also, I wanted to get away from them because all those people hooting at me and so on were making me nervous. I started to walk across the prairie looking for gopher holes, got out a ways and heard a horse galloping after me. It was the sheriff in a buckboard behind a calico pony. He was in a buckboard because he had only one leg — he'd had a leg shot off in a gunfight. He pulled his pony back so that he slid alongside me, looked down at me and said, 'Son are you going to fly?'

"I said, 'Yes.'

"'Git in here!' I got in with him, he pulled the pony around, back we went at a gallop and pulled up in a sliding stop in front of the grandstand. He got up on his one good leg, hitched his gun belt up, held up one arm for quiet, and when the crowd had quieted down a bit he yelled at the top of his lungs so that everybody heard him, 'Folks, give this boy a chance! This is the last ride he takes before he rides with the undertaker!'

"With that, everybody laughed. That broke the tension. I took off and everything was all right, so I was a big hero — but that's the way it was."

There was big money to be won at these shows — and the Wrights hoped to claim every penny of what they thought was rightfully theirs. In January 1910, the first big air show in the United States was to be held in Los Angeles. The only foreign competitor was Louis Paulhan of France, who brought with him an entourage that included his wife, two Farman biplanes, two Blériot monoplanes, two mechanics, and a poodle. He was a well-known aviator who had finished fourth at Reims. The moment he stepped off the gangway in New York, his troubles began. Lawyers acting for the Wrights served him with an injunction to prevent him flying in the United States. The controls on his airplanes infringed the wing-warping patents of the Wrights, they declared. Soon afterward, in Los Angeles, a federal judge issued an injunction against Glenn Curtiss, who appealed the ruling and took to the air.

The Curtiss team won more than $10,000 worth of prizes at the meet, but it was the gallant little Frenchman, Paulhan,

Englishman of good family, had become a champion bicycle rider, then an automobile manufacturer before graduating to aviation. He learned to fly at the Blériot school in 1909, and only narrowly missed out on the £10,000 prize offered by the *Daily Mail* to the first man to fly from London to Manchester in one day — a distance of 185 miles. The French aviator Louis Paulhan won that prize.

Heading for America in 1910, Grahame-White outflew the other pilots at the meet, then won a cool $50,000 at a fair

(Opposite) Glenn Curtiss thrills the crowd at the Los Angeles air show in January 1910, the first big exhibition of its kind in the United States. (Far right) Englishman and aviator Claude Grahame-White, seen in one of his planes (right), took the American flying scene by storm the same year, winning thousands of dollars in prize money. He was among the first to run afoul of the Wrights' patent claims.

who outshone the field. In his Farman biplane, he climbed to an unprecedented 4,165 feet, topping off this triumph by flying to the Santa Anita racetrack and back again. He won a total of $19,000 at Los Angeles and immediately embarked on a tour of western cities. He didn't get far. On February 17, a United States marshal served Paulhan with papers demanding that he post a $25,000 cash bond for any flying-for-profit over the next month — again, the work of the Wrights. Outraged, Paulhan canceled his exhibition dates and returned to Europe.

He was not the only European to fall afoul of the Wrights' legal maneuvers. Claude Grahame-White, a handsome young

in Brockton, Massachusetts, after which he headed for New York and the Belmont meet. Other leading aviators were also present, notably the Wrights, who checked in with their team of pilots and three new aircraft. They were determined to do well at Belmont, aware that some of the luster had gone from the Wright name now that their legal battles seemed to be overshadowing their aerial exploits. Their new racing machine attracted much interest. Rumored to have a top speed of no less than 70 MPH, it was a scaled-down version of the Model B called the Baby Grand. With a twenty-one-foot wingspan and an eight-cylinder engine, the Baby Grand was expected to win the speed prize, the Bennett trophy. But

Record-breaking crowds flocked to Belmont Park in New York to watch the aviation world's finest compete. By now, the Wright brothers were regularly collecting payment from air-show participants in lieu of court battles over patent infringement. (Inset) Surrounded by other flyers, Orville soars over Belmont in an updated version of the Model B.

engine failure brought the Baby Grand down. Claude Grahame-White was again triumphant, averaging a blistering 61 MPH in his Blériot. John Moisant won a $10,000 prize for completing a round trip from Belmont Park to the Statue of Liberty. The Wright team did not take part in that contest; it was a Sunday and the Wrights did not compete on the Sabbath. But the Belmont meet netted them a cool $15,000, plus the $20,000 paid to the Wright company by Graham-White and others to sidestep patent infringement suits.

The legal wrangling was bad enough, but other problems combined to dog the Wrights' operation. At the next major meet at Overland Park, Denver, Colorado, three Wright pilots flew, despite the intense cold. Ralph Johnstone climbed to eight hundred feet, then banked into one of the spiral glides that he had made famous. The brass band played bright military music while the crowed oohed and ahhed. All was well until Johnstone commenced his second spiral; abruptly, shockingly, the aircraft snapped into a near-vertical dive. Some said one of Johnstone's wing struts broke and the tip of his wing folded up.

The spectators looked on in horror as Johnstone, clearly visible, wrestled with the controls, trying to pull the aircraft out of its dive. He failed. The aircraft hit the ground near the grandstand in a huge eruption of dust. It hung there for long, agonizing moments. The band continued to pump out its oom-pah music. Despite stalwart efforts by the police, the spectators poured out onto the field and clawed through the wreckage for souvenirs: bits of fabric, fragments of wood, the dead pilot's gloves, his blood-soaked cap. Fellow pilots extricated Johnstone's body from the wreckage and put him in a car. The band was still playing as the car pulled away.

Aviation was becoming more dangerous. John Moisant, who had won a major prize at Belmont Park, was killed when his Blériot went into a dive near New Orleans. On the same day, at Dominguez Field, Los Angeles, Wright pilot Arch Hoxsey took off at 1 P.M. in a Wright Model B, attempting to

A local photographer captured the dramatic last moments of Wright pilot Arch Hoxsey as his upside-down plane plummeted to earth at Dominguez Field, Los Angeles, in 1911.

secure a new altitude record of 12,000 feet. He got no higher than 7,000 feet, after which he glided earthward. A few hundred feet above the field, his machine flipped onto its back and spun into the ground. Hoxsey was killed instantly, impaled on part of the engine. By the end of 1911, more than a hundred pilots and passengers had lost their lives in accidents. Aviation's age of innocence was over.

CHAPTER

13

The Wrights had expected it all to be different. They had succeeded where others — many of whom had lost their lives in the process — had failed. The Wright aircraft *flew*; more important, they could be controlled. The brothers knew that there was much work to be done to improve their planes, but they found that instead of using their time and attention to perform more research and experimentation, they were embroiled in business matters, fighting lawsuits, doing what neither of them wanted to do. Wilbur put his thoughts in a letter he wrote in December 1910: "Orville and I have been wasting our time in business affairs and have had practically no time for experimental work or original investigations. But the world does not pay a cent for labor of the latter kinds or for inventions unless a man works himself to death in a business way also. We intend however to shake it off and get back to the other kind of work before a year is out."

One example of the "other kind of work" was a device to ensure that aircraft would be stable at all times — the automatic pilot of the future. In 1908, the brothers had applied for a patent on a device that would eliminate the necessity for constant correction of the controls in normal flight. By the fall of 1911, it was ready. Orville decided to undertake the testing, since

LEGAL Turbulence

"I think it would be a good plan to give out an interview in which the announcement is made of suing all who have any connection with infringing [flying] machines."

— Orville Wright to Wilbur, August 24, 1909

Wilbur was fully engaged in business matters. In the last two weeks of October, Orville returned to the old camp at Kill Devil Hills along with Alexander Ogilvie, an English friend who was taking Wilbur's place. Several reporters caught wind of Orville's trip and came over to see what was going on. Orville immediately decided to abandon his experiment and devote the time to gliding. On one flight, Orville remained aloft for nine minutes, forty-five seconds — a world record that would stand until 1921.

Legal troubles continued to dog the Wrights. John Joseph Montgomery was a California-based aviation enthusiast who had been experimenting with gliders for several years. He became intrigued with the idea of powered flight around 1905, and wrote to Octave Chanute for advice. Chanute in turn passed the letter to the Wrights. They were not impressed. Later, Montgomery turned up again, claiming to have invented wing warping in the 1890s and to have developed a machine so good that his pilots were looping the loop with ease; in fact,

Montgomery claimed, he had to adjust the controls so that they could fly in a less spectacular manner.

On October 31, as Orville soared at Kitty Hawk, Montgomery took off from a hilltop in Evergreen Valley, California, in an aircraft of his own design. A sudden gust of wind tipped him over and he crashed heavily. An assistant ran to the wreck, just ahead of Mrs. Montgomery. They discovered the aviator lying in the wreckage, his head pierced by one of the long stove bolts used in the bamboo fuselage. A doctor was summoned, but Montgomery died before he arrived.

Montgomery's wife, mother, brother, and sisters promptly initiated a suit against the holders of the Wright patent. As always, the brothers became the villains.

Whatever the brothers' other problems, Wright aircraft and pilots kept chalking up victories. Promoters of air shows had soon found that it was essential to keep coming up with new ideas to whet the public's interest. One of the earliest gimmicks had been the £10,000 *Daily Mail* prize for the epic

Caught by a gust of wind, Orville's glider takes a tumble at Kitty Hawk in the autumn of 1911

Dropping the Ball

By 1910, the Wrights had introduced the B Flyer. The new design was substantially different from their previous aircraft and featured an aft horizontal tail. Gone was the distinctive Wright canard (as the French called it) — the horizontal flap mounted in front of the pilot that was intended to give their Flyers control in pitch. And gone with it were the days of Wright innovation and aviation leadership.

Once the French and their contemporaries in other countries had grasped the significance of roll control for successful flight, they were off and, literally, flying. Dozens of designs that had previously been failures suddenly became incredible successes. And none was a pure canard design like the Wrights' first model, although a few combined a canard with an aft tail. Wilbur could have flown the English Channel in their Model A — but the fact that Blériot did it first, in a lovely monoplane featuring an aft tail, gave this newly popular design a tremendous boost.

In 1910, in response to a request from the German military, the brothers had begun experimenting with a hybrid design (rather like those of Ferber and their arch-rival Curtiss) featuring both canard and aft tail. It was only a matter of time before the B Flyer evolved.

The result was a superior aircraft. While their Model A had been inherently unstable in pitch, the B was not. And it was an easier plane to fly. But the last technical advance made in their design was, ironically, forced on them by their competitors' progress. The Wrights would never again take the lead in aeronautical innovation.

London-to-Manchester flight. After Louis Paulhan won it, he declared that he would not make the trip again for "ten times ten thousand pounds." Glenn Curtiss won the $10,000 New York *World* prize for flying from New York City to Albany.

That fall, Walter Brookins, a well-regarded Wright pilot, flew 192 miles from Chicago to Springfield, Illinois. Phil Parmalee strapped rolls of silk to the passenger seat of his Wright Model B and flew them from Dayton to Columbus, Ohio — the world's first cargo flight. The Morehouse-Martens department store of Columbus paid the Wrights $5,000 for the delivery — later issuing suitably grandiloquent advertising and selling pieces of the material, realizing a profit of $1,000.

The greatest gimmick of all was the brainchild of the flamboyant publisher William Randolph Hearst. He offered no less than $50,000 for the first coast-to-coast flight — to be completed in thirty days or less. His business stratagem tended to be simple: offer a more tantalizing incentive than the competition. It usually worked. Three Wright-trained pilots competed with all their might for the whopping prize. Harry Atwood flew 1,300 miles but couldn't raise the backing to complete the flight. Robert Fowler left Los Angeles and reached Jacksonville, Florida — 112 days after leaving the West Coast.

The third man was Calbraith Rodgers, whose cousin John Rodgers of the U.S. Navy had learned to fly at the Wrights' school at Simms Station, near Dayton. The 6-foot, 4-inch, 192-pound Calbraith, an established automobile and speedboat racer, promptly decided to take flying lessons, too. He was a natural, soloing after a mere ninety minutes' instruction. After that, he won a prize for duration flying at a meet in Chicago. A month later, he embarked on his famous coast-to-coast flight aboard a Wright EX, single-seat biplane built specially for him by the Wright factory. It had a top speed of 55 MPH and a thirty-two-foot wingspan.

Retailers quickly capitalized on the public's love affair with the airplane. Morehouse-Martens, a department store in Columbus, Ohio, hired pilot Phil Parmalee (above) to deliver rolls of silk from Dayton in the passenger seat of his Wright Model B — then promptly sold pieces of the fabric as souvenirs and made a handsome profit.

Lured by the attractive advertising opportunities, the Armour Company of Chicago agreed to pay Cal Rodgers five dollars for every mile he flew with the words "Vin Fizz" (a soft drink Armour produced) prominently displayed on his aircraft. In addition, the company paid for a special train with a Pullman car and a day coach for Rodgers's wife and mother, plus mechanics, including Charlie Taylor and others. On September 17, 1911, Rodgers clambered into the Vin Fizz Flyer and, cigar firmly clenched between his teeth, took to the air from a racetrack near Sheepshead Bay in Brooklyn, New York. After circling Manhattan, he began his odyssey. He followed white canvas strips laid alongside the Erie Railroad tracks and in less than two hours had put down at Middletown, New York — greeted by an enthusiastic crowd of some nine thousand. Eighty-four miles down; thousands still to go.

The next morning, Rodgers was up early to continue the journey. He confidently poured on the power. The Vin Fizz Flyer rattled off to a good takeoff, only to clip a tree and crash into a chicken coop. Charlie Taylor supervised the repairs and, four days later, Rodgers was in the air again, his head now sporting a bandage, a memento of his maladroit takeoff. A skid went next; at Scranton, Pennsylvania, souvenir hunters besieged the Vin Fizz Flyer, helping themselves to anything movable. Rodgers stopped one man from chiseling off an engine valve.

Near Buffalo, New York, the accident-prone Rodgers hit a barbed wire fence, doing extensive damage to the long-suffering aircraft. Pushing on, he ran into a heavy thunderstorm over Indiana. So violent was the storm that Rodgers had to remove his gloves and shield the magneto as best he could with his bare hands. "The earth had disappeared," he later recounted. "I might be a million miles up in space. I might be a hundred miles from earth. I breathed better when

(Left) The dapper Calbraith Rodgers, sporting his trademark cigar, poses for photographers before taking off in his "Vin Fizz" Wright biplane (right), on the first leg of his history-making odyssey across the skies of America.

I sailed over the edge of the cloud and saw the misty land beneath me." In Huntington, Indiana, he swerved during takeoff to avoid a crowd of unruly spectators and cracked up again. This time, the airplane required a virtual rebuild. Charlie Taylor and his cohorts set to work.

On October 8, Rodgers landed at Chicago. Two-thirds of the country remained to be traversed, and he had only two days in which to do it. The task was impossible, yet he exuded confidence: "Prize or no prize, that's where I am bound, and if canvas, steel, and wire — together with a little brawn, tendon, and brain — stick with me, I mean to get there." He left Chicago, following the Chicago and Alton railroad tracks. Two days later, he was approaching Marshall, Missouri; the next day, he flew into Kansas City, thrilling the citizens — and particularly the children, many of whom were let out of school to witness the fantastic sight. He landed at Swope Park shortly before noon, later flying to Overland Park for the night.

The weather worsened. Rodgers had to stay at Overland Park for two days — during which time the Vin Fizz Flyer was rebuilt, with particular attention paid to the spark plugs that had been giving him trouble since the trip began. Leaving Overland Park, he had a good flight to Vinita, Oklahoma. Bad weather forced him to stay for a day, then it was off to Muskogee, Oklahoma, where he wowed the locals: "To those who saw Rodgers alight and step from his machine, there came a sensation as if they had just seen a messenger from Mars," declaimed the *Daily Phoenix.*

Rodgers set off again, landing at McAlester, Oklahoma, for the night. In the morning, it was off to Fort Worth, Texas. On Wednesday, October 18, he called in at the Texas State Fair at Dallas, having been intercepted en route by a curious eagle which made several passes to look the Wright airplane over. The Dallas *Morning News* reported: "Amid tumultuous applause from an eager crowd of seventy-five thousand persons, Cal P. Rodgers, sea-to-sea aviator, glided down the infield of the State Fair race track at 1:50 P.M. After hovering over the Fair Grounds for fifteen minutes in the most thrilling exhibition of aerial navigation ever seen here, he headed his biplane south and started again on his long journey to the Pacific coast."

South of Austin, the engine failed; he glided to a safe landing near the small town of Kyle. Taylor diagnosed the problem as a crystalized piston. The repairs completed,

Rodgers set off for San Antonio, a weary, gaunt figure. He had lost fifteen pounds since embarking on the trip.

On Tuesday, October 24, he flew 132 miles to Spofford, Texas. The Pacific coast seemed almost within sight. But the next morning, as he was taking off from Spofford, his right propeller hit the ground. A moment later, the aircraft came to a lurching halt, both propellers splintered, skids and wings a sorry sight. Incredibly, Taylor and his crew had the aircraft repaired by the next morning and the irrepressible Rodgers set off for Sanderson, Texas. Delayed a day there because of high winds, he made El Paso by Sunday, October 29, after some trouble with leaks in his water pump.

The first of November saw Rodgers arrive at Tucson, Arizona. He spent the night at Maricopa, then pushed on, landing at Stoval Siding, west of Yuma, when his tank ran dry. Despite his exhaustion, he could feel victory within his grasp. But the unkind fates had not yet finished with Calbraith Perry Rodgers. A few miles beyond Imperial Junction, California, the number one cylinder in his engine exploded. Metal shards hit his right arm like a barrage of painful bee stings. With commendable presence of mind, he managed to maintain control and glided down to a good landing beside the Southern Pacific railroad station. The repair crew's train arrived while a local doctor attended to Rodgers' peppered arm.

Charlie Taylor didn't have a spare engine; he had to re-install the unit that had been removed at Kyle, Texas. By now, the aircraft sagged with utter weariness, its structure prone to every sort of problem. On Saturday, November 4, Rodgers set off again. He reached Banning, California, before loose spark plugs and a leaking radiator forced him to land. He tried again the next day, November 5, but came down with a broken fuel pipe. Determined, he set off yet again, finally reaching Pasadena at 4:08 that afternoon. He came in for a smooth landing at Tournament Park, cheered on by a crowd estimated at ten thousand. He had flown 4,231 miles, at an average speed of 51.5 MPH. He had spent three days, ten hours, four minutes in the air.

However, the trip wasn't over. The Pacific coast was still twenty miles distant, and Rodgers was determined to reach it before he would consider the journey completed. On Sunday, November 12, he took off from Pasadena, en route to Long Beach. True to form, he crashed during the trip, brought down by engine failure, thumping onto a plowed field and wrecking his Wright airplane for the umpteenth time.

His ankle was broken and it was nearly a month before he was well enough to complete the trip to the Pacific. On Sunday, December 10, he hobbled over to his faithful plane, tucked his crutches beside his seat, and set off for the last lap of his odyssey. It had taken him 84 days. He had five major crashes on the way; the long-suffering aircraft had been repaired so many times that the only original parts were the rudder and the oil drip pan — the rest were replacements, and some had been replaced more than once.

"My record will not last long," declared Rodgers, adding presciently that "with proper landing places along the route and other conditions looked after, the trip can easily be made in thirty days or less."

Cal Rodgers was broke. Repairs had gobbled up the Vin Fizz subsidy, although some income was earned by his wife, who had become the self-proclaimed postmistress of the "Rodgers Aerial Post." For twenty-five cents, citizens could have a postcard carried aboard Rodgers' airplane to the next stop, where the regular post office would take it to its destination.

The following spring, Rodgers visited Long Beach again. Some seven thousand onlookers gathered in the amusement park to watch him fly low over the beach. He encountered a flock of seagulls wheeling over a huge shoal of sardines. One of the birds hit his aircraft, its body becoming jammed in the rudder. Rodgers couldn't control the plane and it crashed into the Pacific Ocean, killing him instantly.

A Genius PASSES

"A short life, full of consequences. An unfailing intellect, imperturbable temper, great self-reliance, and as great modesty, seeing the right clearly, pursuing it steadfastly, he lived and died."

— Bishop Milton Wright
in his diary, May 30, 1912

By the middle of 1910, Wilbur had almost given up flying. The endless legal battles, in which he defended the Wrights' patents, discoveries, and even their reputation, consumed all his time. He spent weeks in court, where he was a masterful witness — hardly surprising, considering the wealth of aeronautical knowledge at his fingertips. But the demands of the world of business seemed to drain him; the daily doses of pettifoggery deeply offended and angered him.

Still he struggled on, haunted by the realization that the law's interminable delays were jeopardizing all that he and Orville had worked so hard to accomplish: "Innumerable competitors are entering the field, and for the first time are producing machines that will really fly. These machines are being put on the market at one half less than the price that we have been selling our machines for. Up to the present time, a decision in our favor would have given us a monopoly, but if we wait too long, a favorable decision may have little value to us."

The brothers had plenty to worry about. The French and German Wright subsidiaries were performing poorly. So-called experts were daily dredging up questionable historical evidence in an effort to prove that the Wrights were not the first men to achieve powered flight and, therefore, had no right to sue others who came later. The legal battles with Glenn Curtiss and others — including the shady Augustus Herring — were reaching unprecedented levels of nastiness. There were claims that the Wrights had not invented wing warping and that they were responsible for the unfortunate death of John Joseph Montgomery the previous year.

During this time, Wilbur and Orville began to build a new home, an impressive mansion in the attractive Dayton suburb of Oakwood. On May 2, the Wrights inspected the site. Two days later, Katharine called the family physician, Dr. Conklin. Wilbur was not well, she told him. Dr. Conklin diagnosed Wilbur's condition as a touch of malaria. He recommended complete rest. A week later, Wilbur still had a high fever. He sent for Ezra Kuhns, a Dayton lawyer, and dictated his will. The weeks rolled on and he showed no signs of getting better. Then, as the end of May neared, he seemed to improve. The recovery was short-lived. On May 29, he died at age forty-five, a victim of typhoid fever. Orville was shattered.

There was a public viewing at the First Presbyterian Church of Dayton. At least twenty-five thousand people filed past the casket. The service was brief and without music. Wilbur's body was buried in the family plot at Woodland Cemetery, while the entire city of Dayton came to a standstill for three minutes in respect for its most distinguished son.

Bishop Wright noted in his journal: "In memory and intellect, there was none like him. He systemized everything. His wit was quick and keen. He could say or write anything he wanted to. He was not very talkative. His temper could hardly be stirred. He wrote much. He could deliver a fine speech, but was modest."

Charles Wald was a student pilot at Simms Station at the time of Wilbur's death. He was of the opinion that the "spirit of the Wright team and the Wright Company died with him." Wald felt the death as a great personal loss; he knew he had witnessed the passing of a genius.

Orville was inconsolable. He blamed Wilbur's death on the grinding legal battles, and he reserved particular bitterness for Curtiss. At the funeral, Katharine was heard to say, "I suppose the Curtiss crowd will be glad now Wilbur is gone."

Orville declared: "The death of my brother Wilbur is a thing we must definitely charge to our long struggle. . . . The delays were what worried him to his death . . . first into a state of chronic nervousness, and then into physical fatigue which made him an easy prey for the attack of typhoid that caused his death."

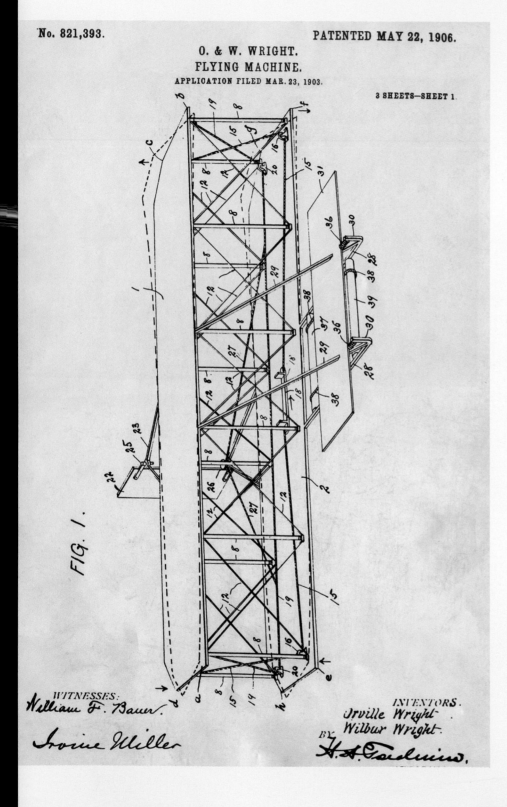

No. 821,393.

PATENTED MAY 22, 1906.

O. & W. WRIGHT.
FLYING MACHINE.
APPLICATION FILED MAR. 23, 1903.

3 SHEETS—SHEET 1.

FIG. 1.

WITNESSES:
William F. Bauer.
Irvine Miller

INVENTORS.
Orville Wright.
Wilbur Wright.
BY
H. A. Toulmin.

Patent Battles

Nothing stands more at odds with the popular view of the Wrights as disinterested tinkerers than their patent struggles — both the lengths to which they would go to protect their invention, and the bad feelings this engendered.

Aware that they had hit on the secret of controlled flight with their 1902 glider, Wilbur and Orville applied the following year for a patent on their invention. It was finally granted in 1906, guaranteeing the brothers a monopoly on flight until 1917. And they were surprisingly ruthless in enforcing it. As aviators arrived from around the world for air shows and other events in the United States, they were slapped with an injunction by the brothers. Some, notably Glenn Curtiss, tried to sneak around the patent by creating controls that mimicked the functioning of the Wrights' planes without impinging on their copyright.

The confusion and enormous amount of litigation generated by the Wrights' patent was caused by one flaw: nobody involved in the affair — not the Wrights, not other inventors, and certainly not the lawyers — understood the essence of wing warping or the difference between it and ailerons. Even the diagram accompanying the brothers' patent application (left) does not explain the principle clearly; in fact, it contained intentionally misleading errors.

The patent battles were waged at great cost ($150,000, Orville estimated), probably broke Wilbur's health, and may have set back aviation in the United States — but the Wrights' patent was upheld. Why?

As Judge Learned Hand asserted, using brilliant reasoning and insight (even though he didn't understand the technical basis of control), it was not a matter of the mechanics — whether warping or ailerons — but of the principle: wing warping while simultaneously using rudders to compensate for adverse yaw.

That was what the Wrights had discovered, and what they were trying to protect. And no amount of modification by anyone else could take that away from them.

Grover Loening, chief engineer for the Wrights at the time of Wilbur's death, said: "Orville and his sister Katharine had, preying on their minds and characters, the one great hate and obsession, the patent fight with Curtiss. It was a constant subject of conversation, and the effort of Curtiss and his group to take credit away from the Wrights was a bitter thing to stand for."

No one was more affected than Katharine; for years, she could hardly bring herself to be civil to anyone associated with Curtiss.

Orville carried on as best he could after Wilbur's death. He assumed the presidency of the Wright Company, but he had little interest in day-to-day business affairs. The only place where he seemed to regain a measure of contentment was in the pilot's seat of a Wright airplane. He spent much time with fledgling flyers at the Wright school. On June 28, for example, Orville flew with Charles Wald for fifteen minutes, shortly after Wald's first solo — which had its hazardous moments because the aircraft had been incorrectly rigged and had stiff controls and a jammed spark retard control. Thereafter, Wald had reservations about Orville, whom he regarded as an excellent pilot but a tinkerer whose notions sometimes created dangerous situations. Interestingly, Wald kept a diary in which he noted the range of mechanical problems he encountered during a few weeks in the summer of 1912.

June 29. Replaced broken roller in chain.

July 2. Stay wire of horizontal rudder broken at eyelet.

July 3. Lost pin holding exhaust rocker arm, causing missing cylinders.

July 4. Skid broken by rough landing in hummocks, break showed skid partly rotted. New skid fitted in two hours.

July 6. Rear truss wire at skid broke at loop in leaving ground, breaking rib and nicking propeller.

July 8. Propeller broken by running machine into shed under power, machine running off runway and striking floor. Replaced with spare propeller.

July 16. Replaced broken roller in chain.

July 20. Connecting rod #2 cylinder broke at bronze casting below wrist-pin bearing, breaking entire piston and cam shoes, the obstruction jamming in crank case, tearing hole in crank case. . . . Altitude at time about 300 ft.

July 22. Take #19 motor to field and install in machine B-14. Change propellers.

That summer, Orville decided to open a school of water flying at the Glenwood Country Club at Glen Head, Long Island, an affluent area abounding in private yachts and speedboats. The idea seemed sound: attract wealthy yachtsmen to the delights and challenges of water flying. It is a reflection of the casual state of aviation in those days that Charles Wald was put in charge of the operation, despite the fact that he had only just soloed and, in fact, had never flown an aircraft off water.

The school had a Model B, powered by a standard Wright four-cylinder engine, developing about 35 HP at 1,500 RPM. The aircraft's gross weight, with floats, was some 1,300 pounds, with a wing area of 460 square feet. The aircraft was a veteran, having been modified from its original form to become a B-9, widely known in the Wright organization as the Hydroaeroplane. A pair of three-stepped wooden floats were attached to its landing skids, the drag from which must have tested the mettle of the 35 HP motor.

Wald made his first flight in the Hydroaeroplane in the early hours of September 9, 1912, taking off from the harbor where four-masted schooners were still to be seen. He found that the aircraft left the water after a run of about two hundred yards. The flight lasted thirty-five minutes. Another flight later the same day had a less happy conclusion. Coming in to land

Instructor Charles Wald (above) and the Hydroaeroplane saw little service before the short-lived Wright School of Water Flying on Long Island closed its doors the autumn after Wilbur's death.

on the glass-like surface of the harbor, Wald discovered that still water can be virtually transparent and provides no visual reference to help the pilot bring his aircraft down. Wald hit the water as he turned, breaking two elevator spars and four wing ribs.

Undeterred, he was soon back in the air. On September 21, he flew the repaired Hydroaeroplane to New Rochelle Harbor, nine miles away. He carried a token cargo of newspapers on the flight, which earned good coverage in the local press — but he made his return the next day, a Sunday, earning a stern rebuke from Orville. Flights on Sundays were still taboo for the Wrights and all who worked for them.

J.C. Jackson was Wald's first passenger. The aircraft performed well in spite of the extra weight of Mr. Jackson. Undoubtedly, the efficiency of the Wright propellers was largely responsible. Orville nearly precipitated a disaster by adding a small lifting surface close to the floats' bow in an effort to reduce the danger of the aircraft digging into the water. During takeoff, Wald came perilously close to stalling the Hydroaeroplane because of the extra lift provided by the canvas surfaces. Much to Wald's relief, they were removed without delay.

On October 4, Wald carried another passenger, C.G. Goddard, for a twelve-minute flight. Business seemed to be picking up.

A few days later, Wald saw a man fall out of a rowboat. He quickly launched his aircraft and skimmed over the choppy water, hydroplane-fashion, to the struggling man. In a moment, he had picked him up. The papers loved the story; it was all good publicity for the Wright school. Even more publicity was gained from a story written by Marion G. Peck, a local newspaper reporter. She went out on an evening flight with Wald, and all went well until they encountered a light fog that had formed with the evening chill. The plane's magneto became saturated and the engine began to miss. Wald found that he was unable to rise high enough to turn into the wind for a landing, so he attempted a downwind landing. The floats dug in, sending the Hydroaeroplane somersaulting into the water.

Both occupants survived, but Wald found himself briefly trapped among the plane's bracing wires beneath the surface of the water. He freed himself and found the imperturbable Miss Peck seated on an inverted float. "I thought you were never coming up!" she said.

Several chilly hours elapsed before a fishing boat rescued the pair.

The incident marked the end of the Wright flying school at Glen Head. To Orville's disappointment, the anticipated rush of moneyed students eager to learn to fly never materialized. Wald was laid off — and became the head of the inspection department at the Curtiss factory in Buffalo, New York, during World War I.

In February 1913, Orville set sail for Europe with Katharine as his traveling companion. The trip was made to finalize arrangements for the establishment of a Wright company in England. After London, Orville and Katharine headed for Germany, where they found that the German Supreme Court had honored their claim for the combined use of wing warping and rudder, but not for wing warping alone.

The pair headed home, arriving in time for Easter — and for the most devastating flood in Dayton's history. On Easter Sunday, March 23, the rains fell amid strengthening winds. Some small towns north of Dayton were already reporting flooding. On Monday, the deluge continued unabated. Tuesday saw the first cracks in the levees; dirty water soon swamped the streets. To the family's dismay, Bishop Wright was nowhere to be found. For twenty-four anguished hours, he seemed to have vanished. Then they heard that he was safe; he was rescued, unharmed, three days later. Fires broke out in many parts of the city. Orville was particularly distressed by reports that the water was twelve feet deep on West Third Street, where the bicycle shop was still located, and where all the brothers' aeronautical research material was stored, together with the remains of the 1903 Flyer.

Three days later, the water began to recede. The Dayton flood had killed nearly four hundred citizens and had cost some $100 million in property damage. The upscale Oakwood area, where the Wrights' new house was under construction, had been spared by the flood, as had the Wright Company factory. The Wrights had been lucky; their loss amounted to less than $5,000 — hardly a major problem for the well to-do family. The only loss that mattered was damage to some of the negatives of the brothers' photographs taken during their early aeronautical experiments. The most serious involved the left-hand corner of the famous photograph showing Orville taking to the air that day in December 1903.

Orville didn't like his job as president of the Wright Company. He was far happier working in the shop with Charlie Taylor and others, solving problems in the "hands-on" way that came naturally to him. Not for him the endless meetings, the tedious correspondence, the fussing and fretting over a million details. He never felt comfortable in the presence of most of the members of the board of directors in New York. He particularly disliked the secretary-treasurer, Alpheus Barnes, a corpulent individual given to telling questionable jokes while puffing away at noxious cigars.

The board had plenty of important things to discuss, for business was hardly booming. The Wright Company's standard airplane, the Model C, was becoming outdated. More

modern designs, tractor models with the engine in front, were overtaking the old pushers. It had become a widely held belief among airmen that having a pusher engine immediately behind the pilot was hazardous. In all but the most inconsequential crashes, the pilot ran the risk of being crushed by the engine. But Orville still favored pushers. He argued that the tractor configuration reduced the view ahead; since the military would be the principal customer for the foreseeable future, and since observation would undoubtedly be the principal mission of military aircraft, the pusher was superior.

By this time, Orville was far more interested in working on his new invention: a device that would automatically adjust an aircraft's controls during normal flight. One day, the aeronautical community would know it as the automatic pilot. Unfortunately for the Wright Company, Lawrence Sperry was also working on the same idea. Orville's system used a pendulum connected to a battery and a vane. Whenever the pendulum swung out of the vertical, the wing-warping control was activated, restoring balance. Fore and aft stability was controlled by the vane, mounted horizontally,

controlling the elevator. A small windmill propelled by the slipstream provided power for the controls. The pilot could set the vane at any angle. In total, the mechanism weighed less than thirty pounds.

In the fall of 1913, Orville installed it in a single-seat Model E with a single pusher propeller. He had high hopes of winning the prestigious Collier Trophy, an annual award for the most significant contribution to aeronautics, which Glenn Curtiss had won for the last two years. Now, Orville vowed, it was the Wright Company's turn.

Typically, he kept testing and retesting every detail until the very last moment. Finally, on a chilly December 31, 1913, he demonstrated the invention before the Aero Club of America judges gathered at Huffmann Prairie. In all, he made seventeen flights, including one involving seven circuits of the field — with both hands free of the control levers. To the amazement of the watchers, the stabilizing mechanism kept the machine at a constant angle of bank as it clattered around the field. The London *Daily Mail* declared: "The news that Orville Wright has made a new contribution to the art of

flying only second in importance to his invention of the first practical aeroplane will thrill the world. When Orville Wright makes the claim that his stabilizer renders flying 'as nearly foolproof as anything can be,' the world will believe him, for it knows he is no talker and boaster." Orville himself predicted that within a mere ten years, his invention would have people flying as readily as they drove automobiles.

It didn't happen. Airplanes were evolving. The exposed perches of pilots and passengers gave way to fuselages with covered sides — which helped to provide the stability so lacking in early aircraft. And when automatic pilots became popular, it wasn't Orville's pendulum and vane that proved to be the big seller, but Sperry's gyroscopic system.

Another cause for grim faces in the boardroom was a rash of fatal crashes of Wright aircraft. The problem had presented itself first in June 1912, when Wright staff pilot Arthur Welsh and his passenger, Lieutenant Leighton Hazelhurst, dived into the ground at College Park, Maryland. The following September, a Wright Model B flown by Lieutenant Lewis Rockwell, with Corporal Frank Scott in the passenger

seat, crashed under similar circumstances. In the Philippines, in 1913, a Wright Model B and a Model C were both destroyed in crashes, fortunately without loss of life. But in July, Lieutenant Loren Call was killed in a Wright Model B at Fort Sam Houston, Texas. He had been making a normal approach to land, when his aircraft abruptly snapped into a dive from which it did not recover.

Orville was convinced that the accidents were caused by stalling after pilots misjudged the angle of attack of their wings. He set to work to produce an indicator designed to warn pilots that a stall was imminent — a forerunner of the modern stall warning device. Orville mounted a small vane on an aircraft. The vane pointed straight ahead when the airplane was in level flight; it had a pointer to indicate any deviation. In straight and level flying, the angle of incidence should be kept between five and ten degrees to avoid approaching stall. Orville believed that if pilots paid careful attention to the position of the pointer, ninety percent of the accidents would be eliminated.

But the problem persisted. On September 4, 1913,

Lieutenant Moss Love was killed when his Wright Model C turned over on its back and crashed. Early in November, Lieutenant Perry C. Rich met his death in the Philippines when his pontoon-equipped Model C dived into the water without warning during a landing approach. Later that month, Lieutenant Hugh Kelly and instructor Eric Ellington were killed in yet another Model C crash at San Diego.

Beset by complaints about the safety of his aircraft, Orville wrote that he found the accidents distressing — "more distressing because they can be avoided." The Model C was a safe airplane, he declared. Then, on February 9, 1914, Lieutenant Harry Post — after establishing a new altitude record of more than twelve thousand feet over San Diego Bay in a Model C — ran into difficulties during his descent and spun to his death. By now, a dozen army officers had been killed in airplane accidents — half of them in Model Cs. The army's board of inquiry concluded that the airplane's elevator was too weak and condemned the Model C outright.

Indifferent servicing of the aircraft also undoubtedly contributed to the accidents. When Oscar Brindley, manager of the Wright flying school at Simms Station, traveled to California, he was appalled by the standard of maintenance. He recommended that a competent engineer be put in charge. The young and ambitious Grover Loening was the obvious choice. He resigned from the Wright Company to take up the appointment of Aeronautical Engineer, U.S. Army Signal Corps. He then infuriated Orville by condemning all pusher aircraft because they stalled too easily and because, in a crash, their engines usually crushed their pilots.

Despite Orville's feelings, the criticism was well founded. Soon afterward, Glenn Martin sold a batch of tractor training planes to the army, and in six months, only one pilot was lost — not because he stalled, but because he was blown far out to sea in a storm.

In the spring of 1914, the Wrights — Orville, Katharine, and their father, Bishop Wright — moved into their splendid new home in Oakwood, along with their live-in help, Carrie Grumbach, and her husband, Charlie. The new location necessitated additional transportation. Whereas the bicycle shop had been less than a mile from the Hawthorn Street house, it was three miles from Oakwood. To get there — and to the Wright Company factory downtown — Orville bought a Franklin roadster. He liked to drive it fast, and the Dayton police soon learned to look the other way when he went speeding by. To apprehend such a prominent citizen as Orville Wright would have been unthinkable.

Orville was no longer much interested in the affairs of the Wright Company and wanted to be rid of it. For the first time in his life, he borrowed money so that he could buy up the other directors' stock. Then he immediately put the company up for sale. It was sold in October 1915, although Orville was retained as consulting engineer at an annual salary of $25,000 — a handsome stipend at that time. He continued in this capacity when the Dayton-Wright Airplane Company was formed in 1917, on the declaration of war between the United States and Germany.

Orville became a major in the Signal Corps reserve but never wore a uniform; he spent most of the war working in his laboratory on North Broadway in Dayton. In May 1918, he clambered into leather togs and flew a 1911 Wright airplane alongside a modern American-built DH-4, to demonstrate the striking advances in aircraft over the course of just a few years. It was the last time he flew as a pilot. For the rest of the war, he worked on an aerial torpedo — a pilotless

(Opposite) The Wright mansion at Oakwood today, and (inset) shortly after the family moved into the house in the spring of 1914. Bishop Wright is seated in the middle, with Katharine to his left, and Orville standing between them.

airplane with a $40 engine. It was unsuccessful and was abandoned after it broke up in the air.

Orville continued to work on various inventions, but at a leisurely pace. He liked to spend the warmer months at his island home on Georgian Bay in Ontario. Few of the locals and visitors knew that he was *the* Mr. O. Wright. To them, he was just another cottager, a pleasant man who was generous with rides in his splendid powerboat.

Katharine spent summers on Georgian Bay until the mid-1920s; then she stunned Orville by announcing that she was getting married. Her fiancé, Henry J. Haskell, was associate editor of the Kansas City *Star*. The two had met at college in the 1890s and he had been a friend of the family ever since.

Orville's reaction to the engagement was quite unreasonable; he regarded it as downright disloyalty to the family. Nevertheless, on November 20, 1926, Katharine and Haskell were married in Oberlin, Ohio. Alas, the union was to be short-lived. Three years later, Katharine contracted pneumonia. Orville left immediately for Kansas City, but Katharine died on March 3, 1929, and was buried next to Wilbur in Woodland Cemetery. Orville's family had become much smaller. Bishop Wright had died in his sleep back in 1917. Of the siblings, only Lorin was still alive.

In his declining years, Orville received many awards. He received them politely enough, but without great enthusiasm. He was considerably more animated when Charles Lindbergh landed at Wright Field, just outside Dayton, a month after his sensational Atlantic crossing in May 1927. The two men got along well; afterward, they returned to Oakwood for dinner — which was interrupted by hordes of sightseers who swarmed over the property, trampling shrubbery and damaging trees in their eagerness to catch a glimpse of the two most famous airmen in the world.

Although shy and retiring in public, Orville was a lively companion within his family and his circle of friends. He had strong and virtually unshakable opinions on many subjects, including Prohibition (he approved) and insurance (he did not). He loved practical jokes and sweet candy and delighted in playing with his nephews and nieces.

His dislike of Glenn Curtiss was equaled only by his antipathy for the Smithsonian Institution. It had all begun in 1910, when the Smithsonian asked the Wrights to contribute one of their machines to the national aeronautical collection. The idea was to exhibit it alongside a model of Samuel Langley's steam-driven Aerodrome. The Wrights refused because the Smithsonian still claimed that the Aerodrome was the first powered aircraft capable of flight. Years passed and, in 1925, Orville dropped his bombshell, announcing to two Dayton papers that the Flyer was to be exhibited in the Science Museum in London. Americans were shocked; some regarded Orville's move as high treason, others as a nefarious plot among anti-American factions in the British government.

Orville didn't care. In March of 1928, he published an article in *U.S. Air Services* explaining in excruciating detail why the Flyer was to be exhibited in a foreign museum. It embarrassed the Smithsonian — an embarrassment intensified by the fact that the year saw the twenty-fifth anniversary of the first flight.

Meanwhile, Congress had appropriated $25,000 to erect a monument at Kill Devil Hills, but the months rolled by without any decision as to the nature of the monument. In the end, it was agreed that the occasion would be marked by a cornerstone-laying ceremony. A second memorial consisted of a hefty boulder to mark the spot where Orville left the ground on that famous flight. But where to place it? In that area of shifting sands, deciding precisely where it all happened a quarter-century ago was akin to plotting a spot in a river. Two veterans of the old Kill Devil lifesaving station, Will Dough and Adam Etheridge, came to the rescue, assisted by Johnny Moore, who as a boy had witnessed the event.

Collectively, they agreed on just precisely the spot where Orville had left the ground.

On the appointed day, some two hundred delegates from the International Civil Aeronautics Conference in Washington joined government officials for the trip to the Outer Banks. It was an easier trip than Wilbur had made in 1900, but not by much. One delegate, Woody Hockaday of Wichita, Kansas,

if thinking of other things — which he probably was.

In 1932, the $275,000 Wright Memorial was dedicated, the trip being made considerably easier for the delegates by the construction of the Wright Memorial Bridge spanning Currituck Sound. Again, the weather failed to cooperate. A persistent downpour marred the ceremonies and a squall ripped the canvas covering from the platform, drenching the guests.

(Left) Buffeted by fierce North Carolina winds, government officials and hundreds of delegates from the International Civil Aeronautics Conference in Washington climbed Kill Devil Hills in 1928 for the dedication of the cornerstone for the Wright Memorial. (Right) Orville, left, Senator Hiram Bingham, and Amelia Earhart pose for photographers in front of the cornerstone.

fell overboard and nearly drowned during the ferry ride from Point Harbor. Allen Heuth, one of three men who had contributed land for the memorial, dropped dead on the deck of the ferry. The ceremonies were conducted in a fierce wind, making the orotund contributions of the speakers barely intelligible. Amelia Earhart stood near Orville, who, according to reports, kept gazing at the distant horizon as

Six years later, the Wrights' West Third Street bicycle shop was carefully dismantled and shipped to Greenfield Village in Dearborn, Michigan, to be reconstructed as part of Henry Ford's tribute to the pioneers who created pre–World War I America.

In 1939, an article appeared in *Harper's* magazine, "How the Wright Brothers Began," by Fred C. Kelly, who had known

the Wrights since 1915 when he'd written about them for *Collier's.* Shortly thereafter, Kelly began work on a full-scale biography of the brothers, to be written under Orville's editorial control. But the book was only half-finished when Orville tired of the whole thing. He offered to pay Kelly off for his trouble. Kelly declined. Orville's feud with the Smithsonian continued until the mid-1940s. In 1942, the Smithsonian secretary, Charles Abbot, published a paper that detailed all the changes made to Langley's Aerodrome in 1914. Additionally, he admitted that the 1914 flights "did not warrant the statements published by the Smithsonian Institution that these tests proved that the large Langley machine of 1903 was capable of sustained flight carrying a man."

Orville was delighted. At last, the maddening controversy had been laid to rest. On December 17, 1943, the fortieth anniversary of the first flight, it was announced that the Flyer would be returned to the United States after the war.

Five years later, the ancient aircraft traveled home on peaceful waters aboard the liner *Mauretania,* to be installed in the Smithsonian National Museum. It was finally back where it belonged. Orville wasn't present. Heart trouble had claimed him almost a year earlier. One has to imagine him smiling with glee. Another tedious ceremony avoided.

(Above) A period postcard depicts the massive Wright Memorial at Kill Devil Hills that was unveiled in 1932. (Right) The 1903 Wright Flyer soars above the appreciative crowds at the Smithsonian after its return to American soil following the Second World War.

The Wright brothers' achievement is unparalleled in human endeavor. After they had assembled and flown their frail aircraft, the world was never the same again. Not only did the Wrights solve most of the basic problems associated with manned flight, they also willingly risked life and limb learning to fly and test their own aircraft. They succeeded where so many failed because they saw the problem as a three-stage exercise. First, the provision of a flight-sustaining surface, a wing, or set of wings. Second, a means of propelling the aircraft. Third, a method of balancing and controlling it in flight.

Remarkably, very few of the other pioneers saw the airplane as an efficient interaction of those three elements. Some thought sheer brute power was the answer, and gave little or no thought to controlling their aircraft if they succeeded in getting airborne. Others sought total stability. It was the genius of the Wrights that they were able to consider the entire problem, not just one aspect of it at a time.

In the Wrights' day, it took a fast ship half a dozen days to sail the Atlantic. Now, the trip can be made in as many hours. The Wrights and their stubborn, dogged persistence made it all happen. They shaped the last century as much as Einstein and Freud did. Although the Wrights were children of the nineteenth century, their approach to the problems of manned flight was essentially twentieth century in character. They did not have to unearth the theoretical principles of flight, as Newton or Einstein set out to explain various natural phenomena. The Wrights concentrated on the design features that would enable an aircraft to fly. By the time they arrived on the aeronautical scene, the science had progressed from the domain of

Epilogue

cranks and visionaries and had begun to assume a certain tentative respectability.

The Wright brothers' airplane was testy and unpredictable, imperfect in so many ways — yet it signaled the beginning of a revolution. After umpteen years, the world had a practical airplane. Immediately, it seemed, countless others followed. And in what extraordinary variety! Biplanes, monoplanes, triplanes, even nine-winged monstrosities like the Caproni Ca60 of 1921 and the twelve-engined behemoth, the Dornier D0X. The airplane quickly became the symbol of the modern world. To travel by air was the last word in sophistication. To be air-minded was to be a part of the miraculous happenings that were transforming our world.

Ironically, the Wright name survived only as an appendage to another famous name in aeronautical history: the Curtiss-Wright Corporation, makers of aeroengines for decades. Perhaps that was the unkindest cut of all, linking the Wright name with that of the brothers' arch-rival.

During World War II, Orville was asked whether he ever regretted being involved in the invention of the airplane. He replied: "I feel about the airplane much as I do in regard to fire. That is, I regret all the terrible damage caused by fire. But I think it is good for the human race that someone discovered how to start fires, and that it is possible to put fire to thousands of important uses."

Flying the 1903 Wright Flyer

The noise is terrible. An arm's length from your head, the unmuffled four-cylinder engine barks thirty times a second. The roar almost drowns out the heavy flapping of two eight-foot propellers just a body length behind you. Barely moving, the airplane claws its way down the track into the swirling wind. You lie awkwardly prone, shoulders and head raised, your hips in the cradle — no safety harness — left elbow resting on the plane to give your hand enough leverage to maneuver the canard control lever. Your right hand grasps the engine on/off switch. Thank heaven the rudder is connected to the hip cradle — you can use your feet to brace yourself against the craft's chaotic bumps. A few yards before the end of the sixty-foot rail, the plane wants to rise. Responding to the craft's small, quick hops, you tug the canard lever. The nose lifts and keeps rising. Quickly, you push the lever to fight the instability. The ground recedes.

You're flying.

Although many have fantasized about that first flight and a few have even tried to re-create it, no one has ever flown a true replica of the 1903 Flyer. But in 2003, that is what I plan to do.

The Flyer was a dangerous airplane, demanding much of the pilot — perhaps too much for someone without the Wrights' experience of a thousand glides in strong, gusty winds. The brothers themselves began modifying the aircraft almost from the moment they were back in Dayton after that day of first flights.

I'm told that someone who wanted to build a flying replica in the 1930s concluded that the Wrights' plane was unflyable. No one tried again until the 1970s, when at least two highly modified versions were constructed for films and TV series shot for the seventieth and seventy-fifth anniversaries. In 1990, an Italian aviation enthusiast named Giancarlo Zanardo began creating his replica of the Wright Flyer using plans made by Louis Christman in the 1950s from the original 1903 Flyer. (Zanardo had already built and flown a Fokker Trimotor, an autogyro, and a copy of Blériot's famed monoplane, which he, too, piloted across the English Channel.) Beginning with taxi tests, Zanardo gradually gained the confidence to make short hops and, after some hard landings, minor repairs, and small design changes, flew his Flyer in a circle, at an altitude of about one hundred feet — something the Wrights never attempted

(Opposite) Giancarlo Zanardo at the controls of his replica 1903 Flyer. (Top left) Udo Jörges' 1908 Flyer warms up on the ground. (Bottom left) This Lear test aircraft was programmed to fly like the Flyer. With the information from this simulation and the data from our wind-tunnel model (right), we now know what modifications to make to our replica Flyer — and what flying it will be like.

with their first craft. But to do so, Zanardo had to modify the canard and vertical tail, choose a different airfoil, move the center of gravity by pushing the pilot and engine forward, and take out the droop in the wings. He also added a modern Rotax aero engine for snappy takeoffs.

For a Flyer that looks right *and* flies well, one solution is to jump ahead a few years in history and duplicate the Wrights' 1908 Model A — as Germany's Udo Jörges did, working from the only original Model A in existence, at the Munich Science Museum. The results of Jörges' work were spectacular — a true, flying, replica Wright aircraft. It's just not the *first* aircraft.

As 2003 draws closer, the world's interest in the Wrights' first airplane grows. Whatever the problems of that original Flyer, at least one group — the Wright Experience, under the guidance of Ken Hyde — plans to build an exact replica of it. It is an ambitious program. How they will deal with the problems of that first Wright aircraft remains to be seen.

Our current Wright Flyer Project plane, scheduled to fly for the first time in 2002, seeks to be as close to that of the Wrights' as possible. The plane's flying success will depend on a body of

knowledge about the Flyer unavailable since the brothers flew. From our work with three test aircraft — a full-sized replica and two smaller models — we have assembled a complete aerodynamic analysis of the 1903 Flyer. After digesting this data and studying the flying characteristics of the airplane — including test flights at Edwards Air Force Base in May 2001 in a Lear jet programmed to flyer like the Flyer — we are convinced we understand thoroughly how the Flyer flew, and what its problems were.

We have chosen a slightly different airfoil and we will modify the canard and vertical tail. But we will keep the anhedral. Our aircraft is what is called "stand-off scale": only an expert will be able to distinguish it from the original Flyer. The plane will look the same — and so will the flights it undertakes. They will be straight and level, just like those on December 17, 1903. There will be no fancy acrobatics, not even parts of circles. But given what we now understand of the Wrights, their aircraft, and how much of an accomplishment those early flights were, that will be enough.

— Fred Culick

Bibliography

Biddle, Wayne. *Barons of the Sky: From early flight to strategic warfare: the story of the American aerospace industry.* New York: Simon & Schuster, 1991.

Combs, Harry with Martin Caidin. *Kill Devil Hill: discovering the secret of the Wright brothers.* Boston: Houghton Mifflin Company, 1979.

Crouch, Tom D. *The Bishop's Boys: A Life of Wilbur and Orville Wright.* New York and London: W.W. Norton & Company, 1989.

Culick, Fred E.C. "The Origins of the First Powered, Man-carrying Airplane." *Scientific American,* July 1979, 86–100.

Gibbs-Smith, Charles H. *The World's First Aeroplane Flights (1903–1908).* London: Her Majesty's Stationery Office, 1965.

Grunwald, Henry A. (ed.). *The Epic of Flight: The First Aviators, The Road to Kitty Hawk.* Chicago: Time-Life Books, 1980.

Harris, Sherwood. *The First to Fly: Aviation's pioneer days.* New York: Simon and Schuster, 1970.

Howard, Fred. *Wilbur and Orville: a biography of the Wright brothers.* Mineola: Dover Publications, Inc., 1987.

Jakab, Peter L. *Visions of a Flying Machine: The Wright Brothers and the process of invention.* Washington and London: Smithsonian Institution Press, 1990.

Kelly, Fred C. *The Wright Brothers: a biography authorized by Orville Wright.* New York: Harcourt, 1943.

_____. *Miracle at Kitty Hawk.* New York: Farrar, Straus and Young, 1951.

Kirk, Stephen. *First in Flight: the Wright brothers in North Carolina.* Winston-Salem: John F. Blair, publisher, 1995.

McFarland, Marvin W. (ed.). *The Papers of Wilbur and Orville Wright* (two volumes). New York: McGraw-Hill Book Company, Inc., 1953.

Mondey, David (ed.). *The International Encyclopedia of Aviation.* New York: Crown Publishers Inc., 1977.

Roseberry, C.R. *Glenn Curtiss: pioneer of flight.* Garden City: Doubleday, 1972.

Saundby, Sir Robert. *Early Aviation: man conquers the air.* London: MacDonald/American Heritage, 1971.

Wald, Quentin R. *The Wright Brothers as Engineers, an appraisal* and *Flying with the Wright Brothers, one man's experience.* Port Townsend: published by the author, 1999.

Wohl, Robert. *A Passion for Wings: aviation and the western imagination.* New Haven and London: Yale University Press, 1994.

Picture Credits

Index

Acknowledgments

Sincere thanks to all of my fellow enthusiasts in the Los Angeles AIAA Wright Flyer Project for more than two decades of collegial work and hangar flying. All of us are especially indebted to our chairman, Jack Cherne, who not only has contributed more than most but also continues to hold the whole enterprise together.

My thanks as well to Ian Coutts of Madison Press Books, who has been a wonderful editor — always enthusiastic and supportive, generously tolerant, and a complete pleasure to work with. This book reflects much of his fine work.

— *Fred Culick*

Madison Press Books is indebted to the following people for their invaluable help during the course of this project. Our thanks to Carol Ann Missant at Henry Ford Museum and Greenfield Village, who arranged for Peter Christopher to photograph the Wright homestead and bicycle shop there; and to Steve Thompson of the U.S. National Park Service, for allowing Peter Christopher to take photographs at the Wright Brothers National Memorial in North Carolina. Thanks also to Darrell Collins, historian at the Memorial, for checking the historical accuracy of Jack McMaster's diagram of the first flights. We are also grateful to Dawne Dewey, head of Special Collections and Archives at Wright State University Libraries, for checking the historical details; and to Professor Bernard Etkin, formerly of the University of Toronto, for checking the finer technical points of the book.

We are particularly indebted to Wright State University's archivists John Sanford and Jane Wildermuth, for so willingly and enthusiastically allowing us access to the university's magnificent collection of Wright brothers photographs — many of which appear in this book for the first time. Thanks also to Nick Engler of the Wright Brothers Aeroplane Company, for lending us photographs of his beautiful models of the Wrights' kite and gliders; and to John Provan, for providing many of the rare historical postcards used throughout the book.

Project Editor: *Ian R. Coutts*
Editorial Director: *Hugh M. Brewster*
Associate Editorial Director: *Wanda Nowakowska*
Editorial Assistance: *Catherine Fraccaro, Nan Froman, Sue Grimbly*
Book Design: *Gordon Sibley Design Inc.*
Illustrations and Diagrams: *Jack McMaster*
Production Director: *Susan Barrable*
Production Manager: *Donna Chong*
Color Separation: *Colour Technologies*
Printing and Binding: *Artegrafica S.p.A.*

On Great White Wings
was produced by Madison Press Books, which is under the direction of
Albert E. Cummings